My Favourite Occupation

The Kodak Box Brownie 620 used to take forbidden Occupation photos
including the cover picture

Kevin Le Cocq

Published by
Channel Island Publishing
in 2011

Unit 3b, Barette Commercial Centre
La Route du Mont Mado
St John, Jersey JE3 4DS

CHANNEL
ISLAND
PUBLISHING

ISBN 978-1-905095-35-3

www.channelislandpublishing.com

Contents

The images on the following page are:- Top: A family photo circa1943 smuggled via internment camp Bavaria to B R Le Cocq in England. Bottom: Kevin's first I.D, Card. Inset: Bernard Le Cocq, June 1940

I, Constable of the Parish of St. Helier certify that the holder of this card, namely, Kevin John Le bocq resides at Exeter Hotel Queen St in the said Parish.

1940

Signature of holder

(a) To be signed on issue.

Kevin John Le bocq (a)

Constable

An Introduction

Nineteen eighty seven will be remembered by many people in the Island of Jersey for two events or disasters that occurred in the October of that year. The first was the great storm that swept across the Islands, Southern England and France in October with cyclonic winds causing great damage to towns and countryside in Great Britain and on the Continent. I was working at Saint Helier Yacht Marina at the time and there was chaos after the storm with many boats damaged both in Jersey and on the coasts of Brittany and Normandy. The second calamity was the world financial crash that occurred in that same month of October, causing serious problems in the monetary world and worries which were to last for many months.

It was in the following month that one simple request changed the course of our lives as it was the year that we decided to leave Jersey, our home in the Channel Isles, to live permanently on the other side of the world, that is, in Western Australia. It was a rather drastic decision to make as previous to this event I was never happy to be away from the Island for more than a week or two. Being islanders we were never contented to be far from the sea. We had been visiting our two daughters, Frances and Sarah since the autumn of nineteen eighty-three and they had just moved from Melbourne in Victoria to Perth in the west of the country. Our next visit was to be to a different part of that vast continent. I was now sixty years of age, possibly a bit old to emigrate, but it didn't seem much sense having two daughters living twelve thousand miles away at the other end of the world.

Later, we flew out to visit them once again in Western Australia as they were now living in Fremantle, the seaport for Perth, the capital.

On the day before our departure my brother had said to me, "When you next fly out to see the girls, would you seek out an old wartime shipmate of mine who, I have heard, has moved to Western Australia to retire."

Bernard had been given his address by a friend who had met the Sealeys whilst there on holiday in the previous summer and said, "Search him out if it is possible as I would like very much to get in contact with him once again." He had written down the name and address of Dick and Diana Sealey, 8, Austin Road, Goode Beach, Frenchman's Bay, W.A. I said that I would do my utmost to find them should I be in that part of the state.

This request came as rather a surprise as my brother Bernard had rarely spoken about his wartime experiences or of any of the people, apart from relatives, that he had met during the war. This was between June 1940 when the Channel Islands were isolated from Great Britain by the invasion of the German Forces and his return to the Island for the Liberation in May 1945.

Looking back to those pre-war days I recollected that, in 1938, he had been transferred from Barclays Bank in Jersey to another branch in Poole, Dorset on the south coast of England. He was six years my senior. I was twelve at the time and attending school, somewhat reluctantly at our old school, De là Salle College at The Beeches in Jersey. At the outbreak of war, in the autumn of 1939, he enlisted immediately in the Royal Navy this being the family tradition and by the following June he was training as a Writer, the clerical equivalent of an ordinary seaman, at H.M.S. Royal Arthur, a naval training establishment at Skegness in Lincolnshire. We now had his portrait in naval uniform framed and displayed very proudly on the piano at the Exeter Inn, our home in Jersey, where it rested for the whole of the war.

The last communication that he had received from the Island in 1940 was a letter written to him by my godmother, May Garnier, a letter which was sent on June 27th just one day before the German Air Force carried out bombing raids on the Islands and the subsequent occupation of the Channel Islands on July 1st of that year. Apart from the few twenty-five word Red Cross messages received and sent at rare intervals, we had no idea of his whereabouts or activities from this time until his unexpected return to the Island with Force 135, the liberators, on May 12th 1945.

Subsequent to his return he seemed reluctant to divulge his activities during his five year absence, wanting only to talk about the German Occupation of his home. It is only now, fifty-four years later, that I have been able to prise out of him some stories of his adventures during those war years, stories that would have made any schoolboy green with envy, at least this was the effect it had on me.

It seems that after signing up, early training and being moved to several positions on the mainland of Britain, his first sea going posting was on the battleship, H.M.S. Prince of Wales which was taking Winston Churchill to a conference with President Roosevelt in Newfoundland in the August of 1941.

Later, in that same September he had orders to join the destroyer, H.M.S. Lightning at Greenock on the Clyde for the four to five day voyage to join the battleship, H.M.S. Nelson at Gibraltar. According to his account of this very uncomfortable journey, he was grateful that he was joining a far bigger ship, as he was sick and wet for the whole of the voyage! For the next two years he did service on several famous battleships and aircraft carriers in the Atlantic, the Mediterranean and in the Indian Ocean. This included being on H.M.S. Ramilles, flagship of Force H when it was torpedoed by a miniature Japanese submarine off Diego Suarez, Madagascar in the Indian Ocean in the summer of 1942.

Bernard and Dick Sealey served together on these ships and later on the battleship, H.M.S. Nelson in the Mediterranean. During one of many actions, on November 13th 1941, they looked on as the famous aircraft carrier, H.M.S. Ark Royal sank whilst 31 miles east of Gibraltar, having been torpedoed by U81 a short time before. Fortunately there was only one casualty on this occasion. On August 11th 1942 whilst on Operation Pedestal, and still on H.M.S. Nelson, they saw the aircraft carrier H.M.S. Eagle which had been ferrying fighter planes to Malta, struck by four torpedoes from U73 with the loss of one hundred and sixty three officers and men.

After this spell of duty with Operation Pedestal he returned to Britain for leave while Dick was transferred elsewhere. He then had the good fortune to be appointed to Force 135 at Mount Wise, in Plymouth, Devon, as secretary to Captain Fremantle, senior naval officer, preparing for the subsequent liberation of the Channel Isles. It was not surprising that my brother was keen to meet his shipmate Dick once again after all this time, if this was at all possible.

On arrival in Western Australia, we made inquiries about this particular address whilst in Fremantle and discovered that Frenchman's Bay was possibly near to the southern port of Albany and that we should drive down to find out. That had to suffice for the time being.

It took us two days to get there as we weren't in a hurry and wishing to explore the forests and sheep and wheat countryside on the journey down. On the morning of the second day we arrived in the main street of Albany and sat in the van looking down York Street at the wonderful sea view at the lower end of the main street of the town, enjoying the lack of traffic, admiring the old town hall on the right and the Old Norman style St John's Anglican church at the lower end of the main street.

It was warm and sunny and a flock of large but graceful pelicans that were circling in a thermal over the town seemed to be all that was different from our little island of Jersey of fifty years earlier. We at once felt at home. It seemed to be a laid back and peaceful small town, not yet discovered by developers and entrepreneurs who take pleasure in changing villages and towns to suit the size of their bank balances, regardless of the consequences.

Still no sign of a place called Goode Beach, Frenchman's Bay so we drove slowly down to a set of sign posts at the bottom of the main street. Suddenly our minds were put at rest as one prominent sign pointing to the right read "Frenchman's Bay, twenty-five kilometres."

As it was still quite early in the morning we followed the directions, through the most beautiful scenery bordering Princess Royal Harbour, the shallow calm water dotted with great egrets, pelicans and other wading birds. After a few kilometres we climbed a gently inclined hill, continuing along a several kilometre long plateau until we had before us a magnificent panorama of sparkling sea and islands, white sands and unspoilt coastline. This was more beautiful than anything we had ever seen before. To the right was an old whaling station with one of the three whaling ships up on the dry as a museum piece. We learned later that these whaling ships had operated out of Albany until whaling was forbidden in 1978.

Our first call was at the local caravan park where we asked the proprietor for directions to Austin Road in a small Goode Beach group of properties. Proceeding to that address and ultimate destination we found the home in question. After surprising the occupants by telling them who we were and the object of our visit we were given a great welcome from Dick and Diana Sealey, these long lost friends of my brother. A year or two later he flew down to Perth and Albany and there was a great reunion and reminiscence of past times.

After chatting for an hour or so we decided to stay at the quiet caravan park. It was without doubt the most beautiful and peaceful position in this part of Western Australia. Returning to the town for supplies we were in for more surprises. No parking restrictions and traffic wardens, no traffic lights and paid parking. Neither were there any signs of high-rise development nor multi-storey car parks, just a rather sleepy old port with a quite wonderful sheltered deep water harbour. We stayed at the caravan park for several days and as Jersey friends, Graham and Miriam Colback also lived at Frenchman's Bay, we soon met neighbours of theirs who proved to be particularly friendly and helpful.

During the next few days we explored the town, discovering that it was built on two attractive hills, Mount Melville and nearer to the sea, Mount Clarence. As property prices seemed also to have forgotten the march of time, invitingly too good to be true, we decided to look around and maybe find somewhere that would make a holiday home. On the side of one of the two hills that comprise the town of Albany, on a north facing slope we came upon an old brick house with an untidy cardboard notice nailed to the garden gate with the words, "For sale, apply within."

Should we wait until after lunchtime? Not a hope! With Faith's usual female impatience, I was made to knock at the door to be greeted by an unshaven bare-footed man with a can of beer in one hand and a cigarette in the other. He was watching the cricket on his television set, didn't want to be disturbed and when we asked him about the house sale he returned to his T.V and told us "To go for your life," or whatever that was supposed to mean! We were learning the Australian language!

We quickly realised that we had to show ourselves around the property. It was an old single-storey house with a large neglected garden and a fine view over King George Sound. Immediately we decided that we would like to own the property if it was at all possible. On hearing that his asking price wouldn't buy a single car garage in Jersey we couldn't resist the temptation and said that we would like to purchase the house. He seemed surprised that we hadn't even made him an offer and actually stopped watching the cricket on the television for the moment. One further surprise was that there were ashtrays everywhere with notices like, "Do smoke", "Please enjoy a cigarette", and similar signs. What a strange household! He was obviously a member of the "Keep on smoking brigade"!

As we were newcomers to the district, we then asked a new friend, Carol Faulkes, from Goode Beach if she would also like to see the property and give us her opinion. She happily agreed and then suggested that her husband Ted, newly retired, also accompany us to give his thoughts on the deal. We were only too pleased to accept her suggestion, especially when she mentioned on the journey from

Goode Beach that Ted had just retired as a building inspector in Perth! On checking the property which had been built about forty years previously he quietly gave us the thumbs up.

The sale then went ahead, each of us using the same lawyer for the conveyance and the contract was finalized without a hitch. He also sold us most of his furnishings at a reasonable price as he was moving to the eastern states and didn't want the bother of attending to the transport. This saved us the work of furnishing the house, of hunting for chairs, beds, fridge etc. There never was a less traumatic purchase.

After a few days exploring the countryside around we drove back to Fremantle to tell the girls that we now owned a holiday home in this lovely town. After retiring from my work in Jersey a few years later we moved to Australia and have lived in the same house ever since.

"Where are you from, Kev? You don't sound like a Pom!" "Strange," I thought. I didn't think that I sounded anything different from an English immigrant, but obviously I did. Tongue in cheek I replied to these new friends, "No, I'm not a Pom, I'm half a Frog and half a Paddy. My father's ancestors came from Normandy in western France and my mother's family came from Limerick in Southern Ireland at the time of the potato famine." "Yes, but that doesn't say where you are from." To further questioning we told them that we were from Jersey, the largest of the Channel Isles, an island about nine by five, with an area of about forty-eight square miles. We also added that it had one main town, the capital called Saint Helier and a few villages in various parts of the Island. "Oh, you mean Jersey Island where Bergerac comes from," came several replies! "No," I replied rather abruptly, "We are from the Island where the small but beautiful Jersey cow comes from, as well as the famous knitted garment called a Jersey and where New Jersey got its name. We also grow the finest flavoured early potato in the world, the Jersey Royal, a small kidney-shape veggie which is also quite famous throughout Britain. Bergerac, or to quote his real name, John Nettles, just lived there, was a great admirer of the Island, very popular amongst the locals, and was a well known actor who made several television series which became famous throughout the world.

That seemed to settle the conversation amongst our new friends for the time being as we were now living in the town and port of Albany where we had decided to make our home. On another occasion one of the crowd would chime in with "Well, where the hell is this island?" With patience and not a little surprise I would reply, "It is the largest of a group of beautiful islands off the coast of Normandy, north-western France. They are geographically French but the Islands have been politically British for the last thousand years. Jersey is only about sixteen miles from the French coast but eighty miles from the south coast of England. The Island is roughly rectangular and slopes from north to south which, in the past, made our main crops of early potatoes and outdoor tomatoes ready for market earlier than those of our sister island of Guernsey. Although French speaking for much of its past history, the inhabitants have always been loyal to the British crown and English is the present language used throughout, although the local patois or old Norman French is still spoken on some farms and in the country.

It was obvious that the locals here knew little about our part of the world. This was not surprising as Albany was at least twelve thousand miles from home, because we still considered Jersey as home. They never spoke about the Island as such. Your comment about coming from Jersey would always be answered with "Oh, you mean Jersey Island", as if it were a different place. A bit later some people would query me with the comment, "Isn't that the only part of Britain occupied by the Germans during World War Two?" "Yes, you're right" I would reply, warming to a favourite subject of mine, "The war and German Occupation lasted five years for us, five long years under German rule and we were not liberated until Hitler's death and the surrender of the German Forces at the termination of the war in Europe. The locals were very interested and seemed to be surprised that we had been occupied for as long as five years. To further questioning I mentioned that I was only thirteen years of age when they arrived and eighteen when they were evicted and, being a youngster, I enjoyed much of the excitement of living in the Island at that time.

Many new friends frequently questioned me about what it was like to be occupied by the enemy. I was asked to give talks about the Occupation as people wished to know all about the happenings during those five long years. There were constant questions about what it was like to be cut off from your own friends and relatives in England, to be constantly hungry, and to have thousands of German soldiers and sailors, the enemy, everywhere. They also wanted to know about the treatment of the civilian population, of food shortages and no news from friends and relatives, of constant restrictions to everyday occupations over that long period of time. "How did they behave towards you, and how about the Gestapo? Were they as notorious and cruel as their reputation tells us?" They were always surprised when I mentioned that we didn't have the Gestapo or to quote their proper name, Geheimerstraatspolizei (Secret State Police) within the Islands. Some would say "Why don't you write about it, I'm sure people down here would find these events of great interest?" So, the seed was sown.

14

Dozens of good books and a few inaccurate ones have been written about the Occupation, but with quite a bit of spare time and a good memory of those far off days I decided to attempt, not just another history of the German Occupation of Jersey, of which I was not knowledgeable enough to write, but to jot down a collection of my most personal experiences, some funny, some frightening or even very unusual, in which I had a part as a young boy with his mates at this a most interesting period in the Island's history. At this same time my brother was in the Royal Navy fighting an enemy who was occupying our Island for those five long years.

Our home was above a pub, The Exeter Inn, the only one in the main street of Saint Helier and one of the oldest in the Island. The business had been managed by our family since the 1880s when my great uncle, Sam Picot, who was married to my grandmother's sister, became the proprietor. He sold the business to his sister- in- law, my grandmother Helena in 1913 and she and my grandfather managed the pub during the First World War. He hated pub life and moved out after the war, my father and mother taking over the management of the pub in 1925. I arrived the following year and spent the next forty-two years connected with this establishment, one of the Island's oldest taverns.

Our first premonition of the war to come was in the autumn of 1938 when my parents took their first holiday ever with a visit to the south of France. Unfortunately, their holiday had coincided with Mr Chamberlain's so-called peace mission to the German Chancellor, Adolf Hitler in Munich, Bavaria. As it seemed to be possible that there could be another war in the near future, my parents, not wishing to be caught in France should this happen, cut short their first ever holiday and returned to the Island after being away for only one week.

At the same time the civilian population of Great Britain were being issued with gas masks in little brown boxes and told that if there were to be another war, we would have to travel with them all the time. Our school, De La Salle College at the Beeches was one of the centres of distribution for these gas masks, and I volunteered to help with the issue as it seemed to be the interesting and patriotic thing to do.

That winter we attended A.R.P. lectures at the Town Arsenal which were given by a Mr Dawson of Gorey Village. This was much more exciting, learning about the effects of high explosive bombs, the dangers of bomb blast, how to put out incendiaries using dry sand and a stirrup pump. We also learned about poison gas used by the Germans in the First World War. To complete the course we had to put on our special gas masks and enter a sealed room where our instructor, Mr Dawson, crushed and heated tear-gas capsules to test the effectiveness of our masks. That all went well and we didn't cough and get stinging eyes as had been threatened if the masks weren't put on properly. On the way out, in an unguarded moment on Mr Dawson's part, Pat McGarry and I helped ourselves to a handful of unused tear-gas capsules thinking that they might be of use sometime in the future!

This had a great sequel on the following Sunday. Pat and I were serving at Benediction in the afternoon at St Mary and St Peter's Church. As we left the sacristy with incensory and boat, following Father Arscott, the parish priest, we crushed and dropped a few capsules on to the hot charcoal to mix with the incense and find out what might be the result! The following few minutes were quite outstanding and highly entertaining! As we moved slowly down the aisle, billowing smoke and fumes behind us, people began to cough and splutter and some, even dear old holy Mary Moore rushed to the door. Father Arscott, eyebrows raised even higher than usual, murmured that maybe we had used the wrong incense! We kept straight faces, innocence itself and continued with the service. Because of the proximity of a possible war, life was definitely beginning to warm up!

In 1938, on September 26th a new Navy destroyer, H.M.S. Jersey, a Tribal class destroyer was launched. The Island schools had to attend a gathering at Springfield for the occasion. I was quite excited at the thought of seeing a new ship but the gathering was only for the presentation of the ship's bell and was quite a disappointment! The ship didn't visit the Island until July 10th 1939. It was later sunk by a mine in the Mediterranean Sea, at the entrance to Valletta Harbour, Malta.

In 1939, a new 9,100 ton light cruiser, H.M.S. Sheffield visited the Island for five days. In command was a Jerseyman, Captain E.de Faye Renouf and we were permitted to visit the warship which was anchored in the inner roads. The States arranged for the tug, Duke of Normandy, on a fine sunny day to take a crowd of very excited schoolboys out to visit the ship. We had a great time, being highly impressed with the ship's size and its newness; it's twelve 6-inch guns, all of great interest. To us, wars were just exciting events about to happen. We were told later that it was from this ship in the bay that the first ship-borne aircraft was launched in the Island.

By now it seemed obvious that we were heading for another war, new warships, R.A.F. planes at the Airport, the petrol tanks at La Collette being painted in camouflage colours and the activities of the Nazis in Europe. This threatening conflict was a great worry to parents and the older generation who still had dreadful memories of the previous war, but to youngsters it was just an exciting time to come and, at the Junior Library, we studied from magazines, aircraft and warship recognition as it was the interesting thing to do.

By 1938 my sister was now married with a little boy, Bernard. Her husband, Frank worked as an engineer on the States launch Duchess of Normandy, and they both helped my dad in the pub at week-ends while I would have to walk down to Greve d'Azette to look after young Bernard. On occasions, Frank would take me with him on the boat when it towed a large clinker built tender with several workers to do maintenance on various marks and beacons on the South coast. While the men were working, repairing the beacons on the rocks Frank would be fishing for pollack in the dinghy while I would invariably be over the side being sick!! During one of these trips we watched Fleet Air Arm Albacore torpedo bombers, now stationed at the Airport, training and dropping practice torpedoes in St Aubin's Bay.

The Second World War

On September 3rd 1939. I came home at 11.00am to find the family huddled around the wireless in the sitting room. They were listening to Mr Chamberlain, the Prime Minister, who, in his monotonous and rather dreary voice was broadcasting to the country and the world that Great Britain was at war with Germany. The family were glum and despondent but I found the news exciting and was just waiting for something to happen, being just a twelve year old schoolboy and ignorant of the consequences to come.

Sometime later, my brother Bernard, living in England and now working for Barclays Bank in Poole in southern England, signed on to join the Royal Navy. This, of course created even more concern for my mother.

A long cold winter followed. British troops took up positions in northern France with our allies, the French, who had also declared war against Germany. We were told that the French had the largest army in the world and the best and biggest tanks. They also had what was considered the impregnable Maginot Line, a series of fortresses from Belgium to the Swiss border to avert an invasion from Germany, and so commenced a period of time that was known as the Phoney War .We were not told that the French had a quite corrupt government and that morale in their forces was very low. Nothing seemed to be happening. British bombers raided Germany dropping leaflets and suffered casualties in the process. When climatic conditions were right we would hear at night the ominous faint rumble of artillery from the western front, rising and falling like a distant summer storm as the French and German artillery would engage each other between the

Siegfried and Maginot lines. Without us knowing, it was a portent of things to come.

By 1939 the income prospects for my parents had now improved, the worst of the depression was over and life quite relaxed. It had been difficult for my parents during the thirties. To commence with, business was slow to improve since the worldwide depression at the end of the twenties, so much so that, in 1938, my father had to leave the Island to work in Southampton at Vickers Armstrong engineering works to supplement his income, leaving my mother and grandmother to manage the pub during his absence. Business then improved with the commencement of the war but returned to nothing with the arrival of the Germans in July 1940.

There were some atrocities such as the sinking of the liner Athena, just hours after the commencement of the war with a big loss of life. There was also a victorious battle at sea on December 13th, my 12th birthday with the sinking of the German pocket battleship, Graf Spee in the South Atlantic.

Although it seemed that we were remote from the war, full of enthusiasm, I joined the ARP as a messenger and attended our depot where the Bond Street pub is located. We met every week and our chief warden was Mr Colley, manager of the Jersey Electricity Company. Others in our section were a Miss Cowdery, department manageress at George D. Laurens the hardware store in Queen Street, the two Miss Procidas, Eric Buesnel and Kenny Matthews, both about my age. We had white helmets, A.R.P armbands, gum boots, rattles for warning against poison gas attacks and sand buckets for tackling incendiary bombs. Our meetings continued well in to the Occupation until we were disbanded when the Germans temporarily shut the

A.R.P. down until soon after D Day in 1944 when danger threatened. The next time I met Ken Matthews and Eric Buesnel was when they were in the next cell to mine in Gloucester Street jail in 1942.

The phoney war came to an end in March 1940 when the Germans invaded Denmark and Norway to protect their shipping lanes for their vital iron ore supplies from Sweden. The British and the French sent troops to oppose the Germans but we were ill-prepared and after a disastrous campaign were sent scurrying back in defeat, the Germans achieving complete success. We followed these events with detached interest on newsreels at the cinema and newspapers and magazines, but it all still seemed so distant from our lives in the Islands.

May 1940 began quietly enough. Business prospects were improving and up to a few weeks before the Occupation, the Island was still being advertised in England by the Southern and Great Western Railways as a peaceful venue for the coming summer holidays! Their mail boats were still servicing the Islands although, at the end of May, some of their ships had participated in the evacuation of the British Army at Dunkirk.

School activities continued as normal and life seemed to be rather dull. Several seniors who had not long left school travelled from the Island to join the services and we were quite envious when some returned in their smart new uniforms. Andre Labbe, one of our teachers left to join the Army and as he was bi-lingual, went into the Intelligence Corps. A new teacher, Brother Charles had joined the Brothers at De La Salle to replace him. He was a rather short, blue-eyed, fair-haired German and was given a rather hard time from the senior pupils soon after his arrival as, by this time, there was a strong

21

anti-German feeling in the Island. He was livid on one occasion when a series of hands doing the "Heil Hitler" salute went past the classroom window and he couldn't see the perpetrators! He was soon interned, very likely completely innocent and anti-Nazi, but that is how matters were carried out in those days. Life plodded quietly on, we were missing an exciting war and very little seemed to be happening. The news seemed to be all about convoys and magnetic mines and rationing although throughout the very cold winter of 1939/40, and when climatic conditions were right, we would hear the ominous rumble of heavy artillery from the French and German lines. We listened to Tommy Handley on the wireless, sang songs such as, "We're going to hang out the washing on the Siegfried Line" and "Run Adolf Run" instead of "Run Rabbit Run" in the sure confidence that we would soon win the war. Unfortunately, the Germans had other ideas!

On May 10th the momentous news was announced on the wireless that the Germans had begun their "blitzkrieg" into Belgium, Holland and France. At last, something was about to happen. The B.E.F. and French armies crossed the borders into the Low Countries in order to push them back, or so we thought. We knew that we had the finest army in the world and the finest equipment! The weather in May and June was fine and warm. From 10th May, when the wind was from the east and north-east we could hear the sounds of distant artillery, intensifying as time went by, as our forces were made to retreat when the German Army advanced across France. Even when May was coming to an end and the German Army seemed to be unstoppable there seemed little to worry about. A feeling of apprehension came after the evacuation of the British army from Dunkirk, which we were told later, was nothing short of a miracle.

As the Germans continued their advance, some English residents began to move back to the mainland, especially when news came through on Friday June 14th that the German army had crossed the river Seine at the town of Quilleboeuf in Normandy. On June 10th the Italians declared war against France and their Alpine forces invaded France on the 20th, the events being classed by the Allies as a stab in the back! What we didn't know was that the British had landed another army at Cherbourg, not many miles from the Islands to continue the battle. The French Government shocked everyone by surrendering to the Germans on June 17th and 18th. Many more French and British forces and civilians in other parts of France were fleeing to ports in Normandy, Brittany and western France in order to escape capture. Stores and oil supplies in Cherbourg were destroyed to prevent them getting into German hands, the black smoke from the burning oil drifting over the Islands in the light north-easterly breeze.

On June 16th the Bailiff of Jersey, the head of the Island, was requested by the British Government to send as many small craft as possible to the port of St Malo to help in the evacuation of allied troops and civilians from the town. Many Island yachtsmen assisted the British officer in charge of the operation which was a great success but the troops sailed directly to England and did not come to the Islands. My brother-in law, Frank was called to crew on the Duchess of Normandy but by this time he was in Overdale Hospital with T.B. and seriously ill.

On June 17th, on leaving school at four-thirty I cycled down to the petrol depot at La Collette which, up to now had been guarded by the Jersey Militia. A school friend of my brother, Harold Tar, who was in the Militia, was frequently on guard, and when the sergeant wasn't around, he would have a quiet word and give me his version of all the latest news.

On this particular day there were no Militia guards to be seen, but I noticed that there were many soldiers in battle-dress milling around, newcomers who had obviously just arrived to take the place of our Militia soldiers. There was a serious atmosphere of purpose with these troops who had obviously just arrived. I carried on as far as the Harvey Monument, and then turned on to the Victoria Pier. Here, I was very surprised to see a large ship, obviously a train ferry because of its different shape and the rails that traversed the length of the deck, which was berthed on both the east and west cross moorings. There were soldiers everywhere, Army trucks and 40mm Bofors anti-aircraft guns were being unloaded on to the quay by the newly repaired thirty-ton crane, and the trucks loaded with troops being driven up towards the town. I stood there in awe and excitement. At last we were going to see some action. This anti-aircraft battalion had just arrived from England for the protection of the Island as well as a machine gun battalion which had also just arrived from Alderney, where they had been stationed. It was something so new, so exciting that I had difficulty in taking it all in. A Jersey policeman with his bicycle approached me. "What do you think you are doing down here?" I replied that I had just come from school and was just having a look around at all the excitement. He then said "Hop it; this isn't a very safe place to be hanging around." I looked up at South Hill. Already a 40mm anti-aircraft gun was in position above the cliff and manned by steel-helmeted soldiers with the gun swinging around and covering the landing troops as if expecting a raid at any moment!

These soldiers looked so different to our Militia who were fitted out in old type uniforms with peaked caps, buttoned up tunics and puttees. Being very excited and not a little scared, I mounted my bike and raced up towards the town. As it was too early for tea, I cycled towards West Park. Just before the slipway there were more soldiers filling sandbags while another soldier was manning a Vickers heavy machine gun which was pointing towards the Saint Holier harbour entrance. I was told later that machine gun posts had already been positioned at various bays. As time was passing quickly I cycled back to the Exeter where I told my dad of everything I had seen. He was quite surprised, a bit shocked and gave me instructions to keep away from the dock areas in the future! At last, the war was about to reach the Channel Islands and everyone realised that we were going to be protected from the Germans and there was no doubt that we were in for some excitement!

The Island's schools were closed on June 18th. As soon as possible, a day or so later, I raced down to the docks to see what else could be going on. I was now in for a bigger shock.

No ships, no troops, no anti-aircraft gun on South Hill. I cycled along to West Park. Still no soldiers, just a pile of sandbags. The Islands had been de-militarised. The troops, the Militia and the Lieutenant Governor had sailed for England and the Islands were not going to be defended. We learned later that Winston Churchill wanted to fight for the Islands at all costs but had been persuaded by his military advisors that this would have been nigh on impossible and would have cost many civilian as well as military casualties.

When it was realised in the Island that the military were leaving us to our fate, so to speak, there was panic amongst the civilian population with queues of people stretching from the Town Hall, up The Parade as far as Gloucester Street to obtain tickets for travel to the mainland. There were dreadful sights at the Animals' Shelter with distraught owners arriving with their pets and where two officials and two nurses were destroying over six thousand cats and dogs which could not accompany their owners to England. The British government had laid on ships for the evacuation, but many people were undecided whether to go or stay and face a possible occupation by the German army. Older people still had memories of stories of atrocities by the German soldiers in Belgium during the Great War, of babies being bayoneted and similar horrors. It was thought that only intervention by the Americans could avert the Germans from being victorious in the near future and that this was the only way that they could be stopped in their tracks. My parents had little choice but to stay. My grandmother was not well enough and too old to travel, my brother-in law was in hospital with T.B. and my sister was expecting another child in December. We settled down and waited for events to occur.

By June 23rd a third of the population had left, and when it was realised that there was plenty of room on the ships many people changed their minds and decided to stay. It was about this time that odd events different to the normal pattern of life began to occur.

One of my pals at school was an English boy by the name of Peter Titcombe. His parents had not long retired from the Colonies and they dwelt in a small house in Bagatelle Road. His mother occasionally invited me to stay there, possibly because Peter was an only son. He was very intelligent and clever with his hands and I would take him empty cigar boxes of cedar wood which he would laminate together and construct beautiful model aircraft. One afternoon, possibly about June 17th or 18th. I cycled up to see him. They were out, the property seemingly deserted, so, as it was sunny, I left the boxes on the doorstep and returned home. Two days later I returned to find the boxes still in place and realised that they must have closed up the house in a hurry and rushed to the boat to depart for England in some sort of panic. We were not to see them again for another five years.

At the same time, about the 20th June, my grandmother was unable to contact her grandson, Eric Morrissey who had a radio shop in Vine Street and lived with his family in a rental house in Landscape Grove, Mont Cochon. His father, Uncle Eddie from the Red Lion in Halkett Place, had also been unable to contact the family so, one morning, in frustration and worry, my grandma phoned for Percy Gosling's taxi, grabbed me for company and we drove up to find out what was going on. On arrival we found the place deserted, the front door unlocked and we entered to find the dining table with unwashed dishes and cutlery, the whole house in disarray. It was weird. The family, without a word, had rushed to the boat in a panic, not to return for another five years. My grandmother was shocked and felt quite unwell when we returned to the Exeter.

These sudden happenings occurred throughout the Island, even some farms deserted, the farmers leaving the animals to be cared for by other farmers or officials from the Department of Agriculture. People were confused. Shipping was still operating between the Islands and the mainland even though the Germans were occupying the adjacent coast of Normandy well within sight of the Islands. A few people continued to leave, others returned to the Island to settle up their affairs and some were even trapped in the Island by the sudden arrival of the Germans at the end of the month.

One morning, a farmer acquaintance of my father arrived at the pub and marched up the stairs with a large block of butter weighing many pounds, placed it on our dining room table not knowing what to do with it. There it stood, about to melt as it was a hot June day. Dad was just as much nonplussed so decided to phone the Essential Commodities office for advice. Two junior officials arrived, were just as puzzled, and as no-one knew what was to happen from one day to the next, and, as the block would very likely go rancid without a big enough fridge, each took a large chunk and told my father to dispose of the remainder. He did this, dividing it up and giving each piece to the locals.

June 1940 had been a most traumatic month for the Island. From the comparative peace of May came the evacuation of the British Army at Dunkirk, and the rout of the French Army as the Wehrmacht swept with impunity across France, that is, until the French surrender on June 17th.

It was still peaceful in the Islands and we still had little idea as to how serious the situation had become in France. After the evacuation of the British Army at Dunkirk and having lost most of their equipment, another army under the command of General Alan Brook had landed at Cherbourg on June 12th hoping to form a new British Expeditionary Force in order to support the French Army in their attempts to halt the German advance. All this was happening within twenty miles of the Island. However, the French government sued for peace on the 17th and General Alan Brook, against Churchill's wishes, ordered a retreat to every available French port to get as many troops as possible back to Britain. The port of Cherbourg was deserted, the dock facilities and fuel depots destroyed, the pall of black smoke drifting over the Islands in the light north-easterly breeze. Fortunately, the Germans bi-passed St Malo at first, making it possible, with the aid of a fleet of small craft from Jersey, to evacuate most troops from that port and to destroy the port facilities and fuel dumps, without casualties on the French and British, who were endeavouring to evade capture.

These troops returned directly to England but our Forces retreating to the French Atlantic ports of Brest, St Nazaire and Bordeaux and other lesser harbours on this coast were not so fortunate. On the 17th, the liner Lancastria, filled with British and French troops and civilians was dive-bombed and sunk in the inner roads of St Nazaire, not one hundred and fifty miles south of the Island. Over three thousand were killed when she capsized and sank. Winston Churchill kept the news of this disaster from the public, the worst since the commencement of the war. The situation was so dire that it was thought in some quarters that this news would be just too much for the population in Britain to bear. The dock facilities and fuel supplies in Brest were destroyed and troops and civilians evacuated on the 18th.

On this same day the British Government demilitarised the Islands but failed to tell the Germans. I must admit that my pals and I were shocked when the Island schools were closed on the 18th. This was a month earlier than usual but we realised that the situation had become very serious in the Island. From the 19th till the 21st there was panic with people fleeing to the mainland on ships provided by the British government. Then we noticed a subdued calm in the Island. It seemed as if the war had bypassed us once again. Over 8,500 people had left on the ships provided by the British Government. The problem was whether the Germans would bother about these little islands. By June 28th, we were to find out.

From June 21st, we found that the rush to leave the Island was over with no queues from Gloucester Street to the Town Hall. All was quiet with few people in the streets of St.Helier. Some of the locals would come in to the pub for a drink and to discuss the situation. About a third of the population had left. As the schools were closed we spent most of each day at Havre des Pas swimming pool, our usual gathering place at that time. The mail boat, the Isle of Sark, left St Helier for Guernsey and Southampton in the afternoon of Friday June 28th for what was to be its last departure for another five years, but who was to know that!

On that day Jimmy Thelland and I went as usual to the pool and spent the afternoon there swimming and sunbathing, leaving at about five-thirty. We then cycled into the town and down to the Cenotaph to see if the queues for tickets to leave the Island had commenced again. No-one around, few people in the streets, nothing seemed to be happening so we decided to call it a day.

It was now about six p.m. and too early for tea so I decided to accompany him part of the way home, at least as far as West Park Pavilion, as he lived at Hautbois Terrace, First Tower. When we arrived at West Park we stood with our bikes across the road from this popular dancing venue and near to the shelter, trying to decide what to do on the following day. We chatted for a few minutes until our attention was drawn to the drone of aircraft engines coming from the direction of Fort Regent. Immediately we noticed a formation of three twin-engine aircraft approaching from the east, the roar of the engines accompanied by a strange crackling sound which we discovered later were machine guns firing from the aircraft. They were not very high and I was told later that they were flying at no more than two thousand feet. I had an ominous feeling that something unusual was about to happen. Suddenly, the Fort, Commercial Buildings and half way down the Albert Pier erupted with smoke and flames, the deafening and frightening noise from the exploding bombs coming a second or two later. The three low flying bombers continued over Saint Aubin's Bay, the crosses being clearly observed on the side of each aircraft and we supposed that they were heading towards the Airport. A second or two later, when we had recovered from the shock, Jimmy shouted "They are bloody Heinkel one-elevens, I'm off home, I'll see you tomorrow", and raced off westwards on his bicycle towards First Tower.

I realised that I had to get home as soon as possible but as everything now seemed to be quiet, and, being full of curiosity, I, very unwisely, instead of cycling up Parade Road and through the centre of the town, sped off towards the Weighbridge along the Esplanade. By this time the dried grass on Fort Regent was well ablaze and thick smoke was coming from Norman's timber store at Commercial Buildings. In a few seconds I had arrived at the Queen Victoria Gardens and standing with my cycle near the railings I surveyed what was going on around me. It was frightening. People were emerging from buildings and wandering around, dazed, shocked and wondering what had happened and what to do next. The road was sprinkled with broken glass from many house windows in the area. A clanging bell brought me to my senses. A red fire engine raced out from Mulcaster Street at full speed, four men and a driver, all helmetless and hanging on desperately, heading for the blazing Norman's timber store. For a few minutes, apart from the crackling from Norman's fire, all was quiet. Then, from the direction of Elizabeth Castle the noise of aircraft engines once again. There they were, the three Heinkels, heading back towards the town. Were they about to drop more bombs? It was unreal; this was not a news film at the cinema or a story from a book. I was in the middle of an air-raid and remembering Mr Dawson's instructions that aircraft bombs were dropped well before reaching the target I was on my bike in a panic, racing up Mulcaster Street, passing Daly's pub and the Town Church, and across the Royal Square. As I reached the gap between the Peirson pub and the Cosy Corner, more gunfire and with a deafening sound the three planes roared overhead in a north-easterly direction. In a second I was back at the Exeter, relief for the family but my dad was still out, hunting for me down at the harbours.

Fortunately, he had travelled down King Street and not across the Royal Square and Mulcaster Street where a Mr Coleman and Mr Farrand, licensee of Daly's Bunch of Grapes pub had just been killed by the last burst of gunfire. He was soon home. As we were uncertain whether the Germans would return to bomb the town, my dad rushed up to the garage, collected his nearly new Vauxhall Ten and we drove down to my sister's home at Bagot Manor Avenue where we spent an uncomfortable and worrying night.

We returned to the Exeter early next morning. My dad was never happy being away from the pub so we returned home, garaging his beloved Vauxhall car in the lock-up at Shaw's garage in the mews for the last time and opening the bar at about ten. In September the car, being quite new, was commandeered with many others by the Germans and shipped to France.

The town was quiet. A few locals called in for a chat but no-one had any idea what was to happen. There were no more raids. Occasionally, aircraft, either British or German would pass over the town, flying low. Everyone had a story to tell, where they had been at the time, exaggerated numbers as to how many had been killed and injured. One customer came in with the story that one of the German aircraft had fired on the Guernsey lifeboat, a well marked vessel, whilst it was off Noirmont Point, killing Mr Hobbs the son of the coxswain whilst the life-boat was on its way from Guernsey to Jersey. Another, a farmer from Grouville, came in with the news that three people had been killed by bomb blast while standing near the slipway at La Rocque.They were a Mr Adams, a Mr Pilkington, and a Mrs Farrell who were standing near to the slipway at La Rocque at the south-eastern corner of the Island when the bombers approached the Island from France and, arriving over the coast had dropped their first bombs. The aircraft had continued westwards across Grouville and St Clement's parishes firing their machine guns at farm workers tending to their tomatoes in the fields, that is, until the aircraft had Fort Regent and the docks in their sights. Their sticks of bombs then straddled Mount Bingham, the port area and Commercial Buildings. This is what we had been watching from West Park. Thankfully, there were no more raids.

Jimmy called the next day which was a Saturday and later that morning we decided to cycle down to Commercial Buildings to see the destruction caused by the raid. I was quite shocked to see the bullet pock- marked damage to the wall of the Star Hotel and restaurant in Mulcaster Street. It didn't take much imagination to realise my fate if I had delayed my departure from the Queen Victoria Gardens for a second or two longer, and how the bullets had ricocheted from the building to kill the two people in the street who had, at that moment, left the Bunch of Grapes pub to investigate the noise. We continued on our way, cycling along the Commercial Buildings, past the bomb-damaged Norman's timber store which still smelt strongly of burnt, wet timber. We then continued on to Raffray's Corner.

The tide was out and we looked down on smashed fishing boats and bomb craters, results of the stick of bombs that had straddled the harbours during the raid. We had seen enough and decided to call it a day and return home. We heard later that a simultaneous raid on St Peter Port in Guernsey had been more serious and that twenty-nine had been killed there against nine in Jersey with many wounded in both islands.

The Isolated Islands

The Island quickly returned to a more peaceful existence, at least for the time being. The air raids on the Channel Islands took place because the British Government had utterly failed to notify the Germans on 19th June 1940 that the Islands were "open towns" and therefore undefended. This was not announced until 28th June on the 9.00pm BBC News, two hours after the raid had taken place. However, the Germans missed the broadcast and did not find out about the demilitarisation until informed by the U.S. Embassy in Paris on 30th June 1940.

Fishing was no longer permitted on the quays as it was considered to be too dangerous. As the schools were still closed it was back to Havre des Pas swimming pool to await further happenings. Where else? The first real shock and sign of the Occupation to come happened a few days later.

We were now cut off completely from the mainland and from France. Saturday and Sunday were quiet. An ultimatum had been delivered to the Bailiff and by Monday white crosses of surrender had been painted on the Royal Square and large white flags hoisted on all buildings.

From the Monday, for us at least, as the schools were still closed, we went back to the usual activities, down to Havre des Pas bathing pool. While sunbathing on the lower terrace at the swimming pool our attention was drawn to aircraft approaching us once again from the East, over Green Island and low along the beach to climb with a deafening roar to clear Mount Bingham and South Hill. They were very noisy three-engined aircraft, flying low enough for us to see the top-gunner in his position on the look-out for enemy planes. We immediately recognised them as Junkers 52, troop carriers, obviously full of troops and equipment, about to occupy the Island and flying low to avoid British fighters. Their three radial engines created a deafening roar as they passed overhead and down across St Aubin's Bay, before climbing again to land a few minutes later at the Airport. The noise had been shattering and these troop-carrying aircraft continued to arrive for several weeks as the occupying forces hadn't, as yet, ships to do the task.

A few days later, I was walking across the Royal Square and approaching Gallichan's the jeweller. Suddenly, from the direction of King Street, the sound of marching boots. Then, a shout of "Eins", then a pause, then "Vier", and then a large squad of steel helmeted, fully armed troops burst into song, marching up the main streets of the town. The sight of these enemy troops in St Helier was a traumatic experience and came as a sinister shock. I must admit that I enjoyed their singing and their music but not wishing to be seen listening to the enemy, I would move into in to a doorway until they had passed. This singing of the occupying troops continued throughout the Occupation wherever they marched, either in the town or country but became far less frequent in the last years of the war. However, they had fine voices and attractive tunes and one had the impression that singing was mandatory from a morale point of view. One particular folk song became familiar to most people. It was a soldiers marching song and was called "Ein Heller und ein Batzen" which on enquiry meant "A Penny and a Farthing". To Islanders who were there during the Occupation, it was known as the I.E.I.O. song and remembered by many to this day. On a few occasions it was very amusing to see a group of ragamuffins marching up behind them, swinging their arms

Das Photographieren auf dem Horst ist streng verboten. Der Horstkommandant.

A dangerous game. A large sign showing German orders that photographs are forbidden and some of Kevin's photos of German aircraft!

Large numbers of troops start to arrive in the Islands

A show of strength with a march through St Helier

and singing in a similar manner and mimicking the marching soldiers. We hadn't a clue as to the meaning of the words although we were told later that, in one song, the words in German were that they were flying against England (Bomben auf England).I think that the Germans hated that song as much as we did as time went by.

A German officer talks to a British Bobby. Inset: German Airforce and Naval personnel relax in the sunshine on 1 July 1940.

The Occupation

It was all so bizarre. To think that in May, the Channel Isles were still being advertised in England as an ideal place for a peaceful summer holiday! A few weeks later, khaki clad British soldiers had landed to protect us and now, without a shot being fired, units of the German Army had taken their place, their field grey uniforms in such a contrast. Thus commenced five long years of German Occupation. In our minds we thought and hoped that they would have departed within a few months. It was good that we couldn't see in to the future. We did not resent being demilitarised by the British Government because, having suffered a minor air-raid from German aircraft from France we realised that we were indefensible. Besides, Britain was facing a far more important campaign than the defence of the Channel Islands and the invasion of England was expected at any time.

By mid July, 1940, St Helier seemed to be swarming with soldiers in field grey uniforms. Their untidy tunics, leather belts with "Got mitt urs" inscribed on the buckle, bayonets, gas masks, forage caps, the ubiquitous jack boots and infamous coal-scuttle helmets, had been seen countless times in the newspapers and magazines since their invasion of Poland in the autumn of 1939. They also stank. Not an unpleasant aroma, just a strong chemical smell, possibly some substance permeating their uniforms to protect the soldiers in the field against lice or typhus. Now they were amongst us, trying to be friendly, relaxed, thinking that the war was practically over and that they would soon be returning home on leave. This friendliness on their part was met with little success except with certain members of the female population, many of whom in no time, had succumbed to the charms of these smart, well-mannered, good looking soldiers. In a

39

very short time these tall fair-haired men had emptied the town shops to send home articles that hadn't been obtainable in Germany for many years. They used Occupation Reichmarks, currency produced especially for use in their conquered countries.

We had one unpleasant episode a week or two after their arrival. Three N.C.Os entered the bar to buy drinks. Dad realised immediately that the sergeant was quite drunk and had the temerity to refuse him. Old habits die hard! It was against the law to serve anyone under the influence of drink! He glared at my father telling him in halting English how lucky we were and that very soon the Island would be full of workers on holiday from the Ruhr. When my dad replied quietly that the war was not over as yet, the soldier became offensive and drew out his bayonet. His pals wanting to avoid trouble grabbed him quickly, took him out into the road and led him away before he would have been noticed by an officer who was approaching on the same pavement or he had attracted the attention of the military police.

During the previous year one of the school pals in my class was a country boy by the name of Albert Le Verdier. His parents had a small farm called 'Kearsney' in Samares Lane. On the previous Christmas he had been given a Kodak folding camera. This was great because, not only did he take many photographs, but we learned to develop the films in semi-darkness and did our own prints, using daylight paper and chemicals still obtainable from the chemist shops. I found it a fascinating hobby and asked my dad if, one day, I could have my own folding camera. He refused, saying that, at the time, we couldn't possibly afford one and in any case the Germans would very likely confiscate cameras as they had done with the modern motor-cars. In consequence, I had to make do with my sister Helen's Kodak Box Brownie, which, though rather bulky, took quite good photos.

One afternoon in mid-August, Jimmy Thelland and I visited Mr Dodsley's chemist shop in Colomberie to buy some M.Q. developer and acid-fixing hypo. We hoped to process some pictures later that evening. On leaving the shop we noticed that De La Mare's gent's outfitters on the corner of Colomberie and La Chasse had been converted in to a cafe for the use of the German forces and was now managed by one of their allies, an Italian. It was now called Cafe Mignon. As it was warm, we decided to take a chance, enter and ask to buy two ice-creams. The Italian behind the counter of the empty premises scowled and reluctantly served us. We were each sold a small watery ice-cream in a silver coupe and sat quietly at a table in the corner to enjoy our unexpected treat. Suddenly, the door flung open and in came half a dozen German soldiers, laughing, skylarking and flirting with several Jersey girls who we recognised at once as past acquaintances from the Havre des Pas bathing pool. We just couldn't believe it! There was one called Jean who I had rather admired whilst sunbathing at the pool, another Gloria, whose brother was at our school, one by the name of Barbara and a very attractive red headed girl called Pat who had not long left the Intermediate School. The last was a slim auburn-haired girl by the name of Dulcie whose father was an usher at the Royal Court. We were shocked but said nothing. The laughing gaggle of girls quietened down on seeing us, so, glaring at them, we finished our ices and made for the door.

It was August 1940, and each summer evening we would hear German aircraft passing over to attack and bomb England killing our own people. Later on, whilst listening to Alvar Lidell and other announcers on the nine o'clock news, we would hear the noise of exploding bombs and anti-aircraft fire over their voices on the radio. Naturally, we were irate. We had heard about these girls, now called Jerrybags or old Pooks, alluding to any girl who fraternised with the enemy. By this time we had also heard about a banking family, husband and wife with two attractive young daughters from La Blinerie Lane, St Saviour who had welcomed German officers with open arms, so to speak, not long after their arrival in the Island. Of course these were all rumours but, in time, these stories turned out to be true. Many Islanders knew about these liaisons and as the war was at a critical stage most people were very angry and loathed the girls and this family for their lack of patriotism. Britain was about to be invaded by these same troops and the Battle of Britain about to commence.

It was at this time that it was decided that I would move into my brother's bedroom two stories up at the top of the pub as he was not likely to need it for some time. It was at the front of the Exeter on the second floor and facing Queen Street. Young Michael Berry, my young adopted cousin, whose parents had died in the thirties, moved into my small room at the back of the landing. It was at this time also that I became asthmatic in a rather unusual form. Bernard had enjoyed the luxury of a feather mattress and down pillows. Without realising it they were to have a serious effect on my health. Although I was not affected during the day, the moment I went to bed my breathing became difficult and within five to ten minutes I would have to sit up quite in distress. The doctor recommended anti-pollen injections, which unfortunately had no effect. I became progressively worse until one night, at about midnight my dad found me leaning against the bedroom wall near to the open window, gasping for each breath and obviously in great distress. It was very strange as, during the day I felt no ill-effects, walking, cycling and playing soccer at school with the other members of the team. However, I was so bad that he thought fit to phone the doctor even though it was after curfew. Our doctor, Douglas Gow, with permission from the German patrol, was driven to the Exeter and quickly gave me some sort of injection which gave instant relief and I was soon asleep. There seemed to be no solution to the problem, that is until someone asked me why I had not tried Potter's asthma powder. I had not heard of this herbal medicine before but was willing to try anything to obtain a good night's sleep. Immediately we purchased a tin of this remedy from Boots the Chemist who, fortunately, still had a good stock in hand. It came in a green upright tin with black writing and if my memory serves me correctly, consisted of a mixture of crushed lobelia seeds or petals and saltpetre powder, the latter being combustible to make it burn. Nothing ventured, nothing gained so the next evening when I felt an attack coming on I placed a small amount in a saucer alongside of my bed, ignited it and inhaled the fumes. This gave me instant relief and I was able to obtain a supply for as long as necessary, that is until later in the Occupation when the Feldgendarmerie tore up the feather mattress and pillow whilst searching for the stolen pistol. It had then to be replaced by a flock mattress and afterwards, with the normal hard mattress, my breathing improved greatly, finally to be cured and I haven't had a recurrence since that time.

We were now occupied by the enemy, completely cut off from England and unaware as to what was likely to happen to us. No newspapers or magazines from the mainland, no letters apart from the twenty-five word Red Cross messages which came at intervals, only local news in the Evening Post and that was full of German propaganda and strictly censored. Magazines called The Signal and Der Adler were on sale at the German Frontbuchandlung on the corner of King Street and Halkett Place. These were illustrated with vivid photographs and illustrations of their raids on England. The former had a version in English but the latter, the official Luftwaffe magazine, was printed only in German

Very soon, the great problem for most Islanders at this time was how to earn a living in the future in order to obtain money to feed their families. States members, especially Deputy Edward Le Quesne were organising activities for the working men and women. Some businesses, like butchers, grocers and dairies were able to continue with strictly rationed foodstuffs and stores that had been hidden before the arrival of the German forces.

In no time at all, farmers were changing from growing potatoes and tomatoes for export to providing wheat, barley, oats and main crop potatoes to feed the population. Fortunately, most of them had stored harvesting equipment from the past. No Jersey farmer, highly renowned for thrift, ever discarded past equipment and rarely threw anything away! Threshing machines and horse-drawn harvesters, ploughs and most of all the horse vans had been stored and were now vital for many purposes as petrol was only used for essentials . Very shortly more working horses were imported from Brittany and Normandy and the Germans also made use of their strongly built horse carts in order to save petrol and diesel. More pigs were bred, more rabbits and poultry were kept and with the former activity a thriving market in black-market pork! We had very little stock or food put aside. Ann Street Brewery had been closed although we were told that the Germans did brew some beer for their own Forces whilst the necessary ingredients were still available. Soon we had nothing to sell.

By late July ships were supplying the Islands with essentials from Granville and St Malo, and one day, one of the Jersey crew, a young lad by the name of Eric Harrison came into the bar early one morning and quietly asked my father if he would like to buy some saccharines. As sugar was becoming in short supply Dad thought that a few packets would be very welcome. However, Eric didn't mean a few packets but a regular supply of cartons. So commenced our dealings on the black market, the only way we had to earn a living. With these useful commodities came, from the ships' crews, when available, bottles of brandy, butter and other items from France which were in short supply in the Island. Thus, my dad set up a small business which enabled him to exchange supplies on occasions with friendly farmers for pork and to obtain tea and coffee and canned food from people with hoarded stock. There was not a great deal of profit to be made but it enabled one to keep going and also to help friends and relatives who were not in the position to obtain a few extras on the black market. Saccharines were priced at one Reichsmark (two shillings and a penny or 13 pence in decimal currency) to commence with but as time went on and supplies became harder to obtain, prices gradually rose. I remember that at one time butter and pork were fifteen shillings (75p) a pound and a packet of tea would cost fifteen pounds, if obtainable, a vast amount in those days.

One morning, I was minding the empty bar and was behind the counter when a lady with a small boy came down the side passage to purchase some saccharines. As I knew little about these transactions I chased upstairs to find out what to do. A minute or so later Dad came down with me to discover that the lady and her small son had disappeared together with a bottle of brandy which had been hidden on a low shelf behind the bar. I was scolded for leaving the bar unattended, especially when I described the lady in question who turned out to be the notorious Mrs Baudains (An informer and collaborator of the worst sort) and her son Reggie, who was a pupil at my school. Although we were not many months into the Occupation she was already renowned for entertaining members of the German Forces as well as being an informer. The only consolation was that she was unlikely to come into the Exeter again and she never did.

In August I decided to take German lessons from a Swiss teacher, Arthur Steiner, who had a small studio at his home in David Place. There were six of us in the class and we were taught by the Berlitz method in which the use of our own language was not permitted. We were taught elementary German, simple sentences, poetry, German Christmas carols, including, "Silent night" and others that I had never heard before. I enjoyed the lessons immensely, found it easier than French, and only lost interest when he insisted that we learn to read the German script! Then I gave up but found all that I had learnt of great use as time went by. It was rather strange. As we six were entering for our lessons, six Wehrmacht soldiers were coming out from lessons in English and the opposite happening when we left.

Now, it all seemed so peaceful in the Island on these summer days of 1940. The war had by-passed us once again. More and more troops were arriving in the Island and taking up positions in country areas. These numbers increased throughout the five years, troops being billeted in unoccupied hotels and guest houses and also in private homes. The Germans also imported prefabricated wooden huts to accommodate the men stationed at the various gun emplacements that were springing up all over the Island. It was estimated that there were over twenty-six thousand soldiers, sailors and airmen occupying the Islands at Liberation.

Apart from this influx of troops, singing all the time as they marched, the German Forces resorted to the use of horse and carts for a lot of their transport, the purpose being the saving of fuel. They were to be seen everywhere, a uniformed soldier as the driver, giving the town a peaceful rural atmosphere. Their carts were of a stronger construction than the Jersey vans as they were used to transport heavier goods when otherwise trucks would have had to be used.

The air battles over the Channel and Southern England had commenced and England was preparing for invasion. My brother Bernard and the rest of the family were somewhere in Britain but we hadn't a clue where.

July and August were for the main part warm and sunny. We were not permitted in the military zone after six at night or at the harbours to go fishing so we spent our free time at Havre des Pas swimming pool. As time went by, more and more of their Forces were enjoying the pool's facilities. Quietly contented, thinking that the war was practically at an end, they were well behaved, very polite and, in swimming costumes looked no different to the locals. Soon the Island seemed to be swarming with these troops in field grey uniforms and they became part of the local scenery. We wondered if they would ever leave. We nicknamed them "Greenfly", hated their presence but could do little to oppose them.

Many aircraft were to be seen overhead during these two months. We recognised Dornier 17s (Flying Pencils), Messerschmitt fighters and Junker 88 twin-engined bombers, as well as the well known Stukas. Junker 52 troop and transport carriers constantly came in from France. In the early days there were two Henschel 126 reconnaissance planes, the German equivalent of our Lysander aircraft, at the Airport. They would often fly low along the coast as if watching out for any irregularities and were extremely quiet, their sleeve-valve radial motors making very little noise with the pilot and observer being easily seen in the open cockpits. There were also two training bi-planes, one a Gotha 145 which got lost on August 28th, while returning from Guernsey to Strasbourg. We were told later that the young pilot had become disorientated in bad visibility near southern England and was forced down by two Hurricane fighters to land safely on Lewes racecourse in Sussex to be greeted by the Home Guard! The other, a Bucker Jungman, crashed near Rozel in the November. Of the two occupants, the parachute of one failed to open while the other pilot was lost at sea. At least, that was what we were told later. When we heard of the accident we cycled out to find any wreckage but without any success. On occasions single enemy aircraft would fly low over the pool, the pilot obviously showing off to his pals sunbathing in their favourite relaxing area at the pool.

The school summer holidays came to an end in mid-August. On the day before the commencement of the school term, Pat Mc Garry, Ron Smith and I decided to visit the school after our last swim at Havre des Pas. On arrival at the entrance to the Palace Hotel grounds in Bagatelle Road we noticed a set of new German signposts wired to a beech tree on the triangle at the corner of Bagatelle Lane and opposite to the mock-Tudor house, known as "Tudor Lodge" which was to become Feldgendarmerie (Field or Military Police) HQ The notices were neatly painted, some with writing in German script and our minds seemed to work as one. Souvenirs! In a second we were up on the bank and unwiring the best of them, placing them under our towels on our handlebars and were soon on our way to school in Wellington Road. Where to put them? We decided that under the platform in front of the blackboard in our class would be a good hiding place and there they went. Next morning we attended school. We were now in the top form, Brother Edward's class. He had a stern expression on his face as he addressed us, "I have been informed that certain military wires have been cut and signposts have been interfered with in the last few days. We have been told that if further acts of sabotage take place, hostages amongst the civilian population will be taken. I am sure that no boys at the school would be guilty of such acts. In any case, do be careful in any dealings with the occupying authorities".

Twenty-two pairs of eyes stared intently at the headmaster's face while three pairs of eyes stared at his feet as they were within three feet of the offending articles! A few weeks later we heard that the signs were found by a cleaner and surreptitiously burned on the garden bonfire by the gardener.School lessons continued throughout the Occupation although on occasions, there was a shortage of teachers. On one occasion a medical team visited the school and everyone was vaccinated against smallpox by being scratched on the upper arm and being infected with cow pox.

One night in October bombs were jettisoned at Bagatelle and landing in the garden of a house called Easton, a few hundred yards from the school, damaging houses but with no casualties. On another occasion more bombs landed at Victoria Village, causing more damage but also with no casualties. These incidents caused great excitement at the school and were possibly due to damaged German aircraft returning from raids over England.They caused a great deal of damage but fortunately, no casualties.

In late August, Ron Smith, Pat Mc Garry, Nev Le Boutillier and I decided to cycle to the Airport to see what was going on out there and to have a look at some of the aircraft which we saw frequently flying over the town. As we approached the airfield we saw several planes hidden in fields around, one a Junker 88 bomber which I photographed, its markings covered with camouflage material to disguise it from the air. On the Quennevais Road a prominent sign forbidding photography was clearly marked but as we couldn't understand the language, we looked the other way and just ignored it. I kept my sister's Kodak Box Brownie hidden in the cycle basket under a towel as we proceeded along the Rue Caree and on to Water Lane. Here we placed our bikes against the grassy bank and climbed up a muddy track to the airport perimeter where we surveyed all before us. This was fantastic! Right up to the airport perimeter and without a guard in sight. As it was obvious that we could have been seen from the airport building I got Ron Smith to move slightly to the front and he took a quick photo of the Junker 52 troop carrier which was standing in front of the hanger. There were more aircraft further away but too far for a photo. We then noticed, to our right, not a hundred yards away, a Junker 88 bomber, partly camouflaged. Out again with the camera, a quick snap and then we noticed a sentry behind the tail but fortunately facing away from us. At that moment we saw a farm labourer stalking quickly our way, his hoe over his shoulder. His comment we will never forget, it seemed so funny at the time. "My Gord, if the Gord catches you, Gord help you!" and then turned abruptly and went back to his hoeing. Not wishing to take any more chances we soon scrambled down the bank, still chuckling, on to our cycles and raced home.

A few days later I achieved my next ambition, to photograph German troops marching up Queen Street. This was a frequent occurrence at the beginning of the Occupation and as soon as I heard the singing from approaching troops I positioned myself behind the curtain in our first floor lounge. Unfortunately, my grandmother was there at the time and was determined that I wouldn't get into trouble. As the troops arrived outside, I dodged her, stuck the camera behind the curtain and, without the use of the viewfinder took a quick photo. She was furious and I just hoped that I had been successful. I was to find out later that night when I developed the film in the scullery as soon as it was dark enough. The next evening I was able to make a few prints and handed some around to my pals at school. I was thirteen at the time. I frequently tried to take photographs of troops and their vehicles from the first floor window, that is when my grandmother wasn't around. On one occasion I was peering through the viewfinder at one soldier when I noticed that he had stopped and looked up at me in the window. He stood there grinning at me, arms akimbo waiting to be photographed. I had quite a shock, took a quick snap and soon disappeared. Unfortunately, this was one of the pictures destroyed by my parents at the when I seemed to be always in trouble with the German police.

My British Army First-Aid Kit

One dull Thursday, early in September, a school pal, Sonny Egre, invited me up to his father's farm at the top of Beaumont Hill as he had something interesting to show me. As it was too cool for swimming and I had nowhere to fish, I decided to take him up on his offer. Leaving the Exeter at about two I cycled westwards along Victoria Avenue. When I arrived at Millbrook, I noticed a park on the right that I had never seen before, with the gates wide open so I decided to cross over to have a look inside. I passed the now neglected gardens, walking towards the inner road where I intended to continue my journey. What occurred next, an insignificant event at the time, was to affect our family throughout the Occupation. As I approached the inner gate I saw two young boys playing at the half-filled boating pool with two adults, possibly their parents, watching a short distance away. After a few moments the parents approached me and chatted quite pleasantly about this and that. I suppose that I was flattered that adults would wish to talk to someone of my age. In those few short moments they said that they had come to Jersey just before the war to buy a hotel and had been trapped by the rapid arrival of the German Forces. I told them how sorry I was, promptly forgot all about them, and continued on my way to the farm.

In about twenty minutes I had cycled up Beaumont Hill and Eggo, as Sunny Egre was nicknamed, met me at the gate and led me to one of his father's barns. The big door was closed but he soon opened it to expose what looked like a brand-new, camouflaged British Army lorry, in splendid condition, very likely captured during the rapid German advance across France.

No Germans around so we clambered over the vehicle hunting for souvenirs. No guns, ammunition or anything that exciting, but behind the driver's seat, in a special slot, a large gun-metal field first-aid kit marked with a Red Cross on a white background. It had been untouched, packed to the top with bandages, dressings and surgical instruments for wounds sustained in battle. As Eggo wasn't interested I didn't see why I shouldn't take it as a souvenir. Wrapping it in a bit of sacking, I fixed it to the carrier of my bike and proceeded to take it home and put it in its pride of place at the top of my bedroom chest of drawers, there to reside until late in the Occupation. In September 1942, when the German Field Police searched the Exeter for the first time, they examined the first aid box, not knowing it's origin, left it in place and passed no comment, according to my father. I didn't know about this as I was in jail!

Two or three weeks later I met the family that I had met at Millbrook as my mother and I were leaving St Mary and St Peter's Church after Sunday Mass. I had explained their predicament to my parents and so my mother, always kind to everyone, invited the family to Sunday lunch in the week to come. So commenced a casual friendship and the four were invited home on many occasions whenever we had a piece of black-market pork or a chicken for Sunday lunch. In the September our practically new Vauxhall Ten car was taken by the German authorities and, I think that my father was paid some form of compensation.

As the year was coming to an end we heard that our wood and corrugated iron bungalow on Gorey Common, our summer retreat, was likely to be removed in the New Year. It was in the line of fire for future gun emplacements and a possible anti-tank wall likely to be built. My dad decided to move it before that happened. With the help of his pal, Jimmy Langlois of Val Poucin Farm, Longueville they made several trips to Gorey with the horse and van, dismantled as much as possible, transported and stored the timber in our now empty cellar at the Exeter, Jimmy taking the corrugated iron and surplus timber for the farm. The wood proved to be of great use during the coming harsh winter when fuel was in short supply.

In the following spring the Germans removed or destroyed the remainder of the bungalows and, as they had been constructed on the Grouville tenant's land we were never permitted to re-build them after the war as new building regulations prohibited this type of development. Some Islanders thought that this was one of the good deeds the Germans carried out during their five year stay! We did not!

By mid-August more big guns were being brought into the Island, although the heavier 88mm anti-aircraft guns weren't installed until the New Year when the battery, newly positioned at Fort Regent, fired for the first time. The volume of noise was quite frightening as the Exeter was just beneath the cliffs of the Fort. The first time I was made aware of their presence occurred when, on my way home from attending our air-raid post in Bond Street, the hum of aircraft engines could suddenly be heard from R.A.F bombers flying south, then bright flashes and deafening crashes came from above where the Germans had recently placed the new anti-aircraft battery. A little later one could hear the patter of small pieces of shrapnel raining down on the town roof-tops and I soon took cover, realising that a large piece of shrapnel or shell cap would kill you if it landed on your head. We learned later that the R.A.F. bombers would cross the Island when on a raid to the port of St Nazaire but not when they raided the port of Brest. There were many such raids on St Nazaire as it was there that the Germans had taken possession of a giant dry dock, part of the

French naval docks and big enough for their largest warships. These nightly flak barrages were very disturbing especially for my Gran, now often confused, who, one morning, following the nightly barrage, came out with the comment about the previous night's upset with the amusing statement, "Were they R.A.F. planes or some of ours?"As time went on, she found the increasing numbers of occupying troops very worrying and wondered if the problems that had occurred from 1914 until 1918 would be repeated by the German troops.

She and her husband, Edward Morrissey had held the pub licence from 1913 and throughout the First World War. Life for publicans in licensed premises was far from peaceful during those war years as there were frequent fights and disturbances between these battle worn troops when on leave, so much so that on occasions certain sections of British and Colonial forces would be barred from many of the town's pubs. There was really no need for her to have worried as this never happened with the German troops, as there was little or no alcohol for sale to civilians and the soldiers were strictly disciplined and did their drinking in their own clubs and Soldatenheime (Soldiers' Homes), away from the view of the civilian population. She had no need to worry.

As time went by more and more troops would arrive in the Island. It was never possible to relax during those five long years of Occupation. You never knew from week to week what new instructions would appear in the Evening Post. Would the rations be cut even more? When would your property be searched again by the feared Feldgendarmerie? Every night of those five years one had to be off the streets by ten or eleven at night and not allowed out until six or seven the following morning. If you lived in the town the patrols could be heard at regular intervals monitoring the streets and it would be dangerous being out after curfew. We also wondered constantly how the relatives and friends on the mainland were coping with the blitz and the bombing of provincial towns.

It was often said that what women missed most was a good cup of tea and the men the odd pint or two of good ale, but all these things had to wait. Neither was of interest to me at my age, but I was always hungry and missed sweets and chocolate which were always in short supply and for the most part unobtainable.

One ruse we soon discovered after a while was to hide the forbidden crystal radio set in the copious pocket of my grandmother's pinafore although the look of guilt on her face would have given her away immediately should the Germans have questioned her. However, she survived and enjoyed meeting her old locals once again when they returned gradually after the Liberation. Her funniest comment occurred on one occasion when one of the returning locals came out with the question, "Well Lena, how did you cope with all those Jerries using your pub? Didn't they cause trouble at times and weren't you afraid?" Without much thought she replied, "Well Bill, they weren't much trouble as they rarely drank in the town and besides, they were very disciplined and afraid of being sent to the Russian front and therefore were well behaved." And with a smile, as if remembering pub life in the First World War pensively added, "To be honest, I would rather have five years of German Occupation than five minutes of Allied troops if trouble is what you are referring to!" Of course my Gran was not being critical of the soldiers who were sent to Jersey on leave during the First World War as she realised what dreadful privations these British and Colonial troops had been through in the trenches on the Western Front. It was also too far for many of them to return home on leave. She had lived at the Exeter during both world wars and her memories of the pub during those troublesome times were quite vivid.

From 1941 one would frequently see big artillery weapons towed through the town by large half-track vehicles called Borgwards, if my memory serves me right and placed at various sites in the Island. In summer the half-tracks would cause considerable damage to the soft tarmac when they turned at the corners.

In September 1940 the daylight raids on Britain were waning, many of the aircraft at the Airport leaving the Island for other destinations. More troops and artillery came to the Island as the Germans were having other ideas concerning the invasion of Britain.

It was about this time that my dad began helping friends and relatives who were finding it difficult coping with the ever shortening rations. My two aunts who lived at 6, The Parade were the first two to be looked after. Eileen Nicolle, the daughter gave my father her new Sunbeam bicycle so that he could get around attending to various people. He also visited the Garniers, long time family friends who lived in St Clement's Gardens and also an elderly English couple by the name of Anderton who lived on the sea front at Greve d'Azette. My mother and I used to cycle to Rozel Valley with a little butter and a few eggs to visit my aunt Muriel Izalene de Gruchy who lived alone in a little cottage called "Cintra". We were quite shocked to see that she cooked her meagre meals over a griddle and open fire of twigs. She was becoming very thin, her husband, a sea captain on the Clan Lines was away fighting the war. They owned this cottage, several other properties and two farms in the same parish, so one day my mother, noticing how thin and emaciated Muriel had become said to her, "Muriel, why don't you buy a little black-market butter to help with your rations?" As butter was now five shillings a pound, Muriel turned to my mother quite horrified and said in all seriousness in her lovely sing-song Jersey country accent, "Ah, but my poor Hilda, when Phlip comes home after the war, he is going to want to know where the money went to!" and so she managed on her rations and what we were able to take her. She passed away six months after the Liberation, "of a chill and malnutrition", the doctor said. We Jerriais were not renowned for being thrifty for no reason at all!

Our first Occupation Christmas was soon approaching, ideas of peace were fading as the news became worse instead of better. For this first Christmas there were still supplies to be obtained, extra rations, black-market pork and chickens and even stores of liquor, obviously kept back for a special occasion. As a concession, the German authorities extended the curfew on Christmas and New Year's Eve to enable the population to attend religious services should they wish to do so. My mother decided that she and I would attend Midnight Mass at St Thomas' Church as there wasn't a service at our church in Vauxhall Street. On Christmas Eve, a cold, still, moonlight night we left the pub at about eleven forty to walk to Mass, and arrived about fifteen minutes later. There were quite a few civilians to be seen on the way, noisy, staggering around, some overfull of the Christmas spirit and well under the influence. Obviously not a shortage of alcohol in some quarters! There were no German soldiers to be seen, not even the usual patrols. As we approached the church and made to enter by the side steps we were surprised at the volume of singing emanating from the building and found it packed, not just by some of the local Catholics but by hundreds of German soldiers, so many that we had to find a pew in a side aisle to participate in the Mass. The singing was wonderful, their fine male voices harmonising the many hymns as well as German Christmas carols. I cannot hear "Stille Nacht, Heilige

Nacht" and "Oh du Froelige, oh du Selige," without being transported back to that memorable occasion. Not only did we wish that they were back in their own country but I am sure that they would have preferred to be home with their families on this occasion rather than in a strange island in the bay of Mont Saint Michel.

New Year's Eve was a much more subdued affair. The war news was far from encouraging and it was going to be a far longer occupation than we had anticipated. We hadn't heard from my brother or any others of the family who had evacuated to England and had no idea where they were or how they were coping in a strange country. Thus, 1940, a most momentous year, came to an end.

The first few months of 1941 dragged interminably on. It was a long cold winter, food and commodity rations were decreased and more and more regulations from the governing authorities were announced in the Evening Post, as well as the war news as seen from the German propaganda point of view.

One startling item of news shocked Islanders in March of 1941. We heard that a party of young Frenchmen had escaped in a small craft from the French mainland, and landed in Saint Peter Port, Guernsey. Seeing the writing on notice boards in English, they marched up the pier singing the Marseillaise, the French national anthem, thinking that they had landed in the Isle of Wight. At least, that was what we were told. They were captured, tried by German court martial and their young leader, Francois Scornet, sentenced to death. He was later brought over to Jersey and shot by firing squad at St Ouen's Manor.

One small bonus at the time was the arrival of Red Cross letters from the mainland in February. We heard from relatives and also, later in the Occupation, a message from my brother Bernard who was in the Royal Navy. In few words he mentioned that he had joined the Nelson family and as we didn't know any people by the name of Nelson, my Dad, who had also been in the Royal Navy in the First World War deduced that he could have joined H.M.S. Nelson, a British battleship. Later this was proved to be correct because at the time he had joined the ship at Gibraltar for the Pedestal convoy to relieve the Island of Malta. On one occasion when the German police were searching the pub, one officer saw my brother's photo in naval uniform on the piano; he turned to my father and said "Your son?" and when my father nodded he replied, "It is a good thing that he is fighting for his country."

Just as the winter of 1940/41 was ending, so we were coming to the end of the timber from the bungalow which had been stored in the cellar. As the last planks were removed and chopped up, to his surprise my dad exposed a full crate of White Shield Worthington ale. What bliss! This treasure was in perfect condition and quickly consumed by my father and close friends. Also, at this time, our new friends from the mainland asked us if they could store some mattresses in the cellar which was now empty. Dad couldn't see any harm in that, so, the following week the gentleman turned up with the two boys and a handcart, piled high with these mattresses. The front hatch was opened and the mattresses stored below. The gentleman concerned also mentioned to Dad that, as his money and property were on the mainland, they were quite short of cash and whether Dad could help him to pay his school fees. Ignoring his oft repeated message to me," Neither a borrower nor a lender be", as there was a regular supply of Reichsmarks coming in, Dad was able to give him enough cash periodically to keep the boys at school.

The Germans were now beginning to fortify the Islands with more armaments arriving weekly from France. On April 20th the film "Victory in the West," was shown at the Forum Cinema for the German Forces and I managed to sneak up and photograph the front of the cinema with the swastikas and title," Victory in the West," in English for our benefit, I suppose.

I was still intent on getting hold of a better camera but without much help from the family. One day, however my dad said to me, "Do you still want a camera?" Full of enthusiasm and hope, I replied in the affirmative. "Well", he said, "I have got you a job for the summer months and you will be able to save your wages and buy one. You can go and work for my friend, Harold Bree, on his farm at Fauvic." I think that my dad had an ulterior motive which was finding me something to do with my spare time to keep me out of trouble! Not having had a job before it sounded too good to be true but as soon as we broke up for the summer holidays, on the following Monday, I was up at seven and cycling on the inner road to Fauvic crossroads as instructed.

There were about ten or eleven farm labourers working for Harold at the time. I found the work hard but as I was getting sufficient food and was young it did more good than harm. There was one old chap called Le Clercq, an Irishman by the name of Pat O' Toole, Ted Luce, the foreman, who I believe was Harold's brother-in-law and others whose names I can't remember now. There were also two younger brothers, the Le Clercq boys, the older Don, fair-haired, blue-eyed and as strong as an ox and his younger brother Cyril, called Sam for some odd reason. They were about eighteen to twenty years old. I was to work with the two of them during my time on the farm.

There were no Jersey cattle at Fauvic Farm. It was a grower's estate. All fields in pre-war days produced early potatoes and outdoor tomatoes for export. Suddenly, in June 1940, the market for these products dried up. Then, with the arrival of the Army of Occupation it became necessary to change cultivation to the growing of wheat, barley, oats and main crop potatoes. Every possible square yard had to be cultivated, even the tiny patches of land on the Verclut headland, just above Fauvic crossroads. Later, these tiny paddocks had to be cut with a sickle or scythe by the three of us, stooked, and when dry, collected with the horse and van which was very difficult on the steep cotils. There were some greenhouses on the farm but not in use as fuel was unobtainable in order to operate them in colder months. There were also two horses, one a twenty year old grey mare and a young bad tempered French gelding. Apart from that there were just chickens and rabbits.

One morning, Harold said to Don, "Take Kevin with you in the van and go to Norman's store on Commercial Buildings. They have a pile of empty barrels belonging to us. If we don't pick them up, somebody else will and they will soon be lost." Well, we set off at a brisk trot along the inner road, I enjoying every moment, Don well in control of the stroppy French horse. At Norman's we stacked the barrels as high as possible and Don lashed them down well so that they wouldn't move. We then set off back to the farm, through the town, past the Jersey Sports Stadium, our pre-war roller skating rink, turned left at Plat Douet Road and on to the Inner Road. Don then noticed that some of the barrels were working loose at the back. Handing me the reins with instructions to keep a firm grip, he proceeded to climb up on top of the load and moved to the back to make it secure. Earlier in the morning, on the way to town, we had noticed that the Germans were having manoeuvres on the golf course but paid little notice to those goings on. Now, as the van arrived at the same area and opposite my aunt's house at 23, St Clement's Gardens, there were German soldiers everywhere with rifles and machine guns, running from trench to trench on the green golf course to our left. While Don was at the back of the load, one of the Germans opened fire with a machine-gun. The unexpected loud noise made me jump and startled the horse which reared up with fright. In a second it had bolted leaving me petrified and hanging on to the reins and scared out of my mind as the loaded van raced along the inner road towards Samares Manor. Don yelled from the back," Hang on Kev. I'm coming," and promptly launched himself from the top of the load on to the horse's back, grabbing the reins and swiftly dragging him to a halt to my great relief. I think his leap would have done credit to a Hollywood stunt man in a cowboy film but I was still shaking a bit when we arrived back at the farm.

I worked with Don and Cyril throughout those warm wartime summer months. It was very peaceful with now few aircraft overhead. One exception was a Heinkel 111 reconnaissance aircraft which flew regularly quite high in the azure sky. On occasions we had to weed fields of swedes and mangolds, the worst job I had been given on the farm. On another occasion we had to help with the creation of a huge stack of oats in the farm-yard, waiting for the time to thresh when our turn came around. I found it extremely interesting, the skill of these farm workers able to create a perfect stack, something not carried out for generations. At a later date, I visited a farm in the west of the Island and watched a large threshing machine powered by an old steam portable engine, a wonderful sight, the field full of horses and vans, piled high with the harvest from various farms in the district.

Most farms now were growing their full quota of wheat, barley and oats and the farmers knew that the stacks had to be dry before harvesting. Any damp areas, if left the ricks, were likely to burst into flames with spontaneous combustion and destroy the whole stack. Harold was particularly careful as we had heard of several farmers who had lost their entire crop because of fire.

On one occasion, the three of us were having a sandwich during the mid-day break. It had rained during the night and we were moving the stooks of barley. To our surprise the short stubble seemed to be moving, as if alive. On looking closer we saw that there were thousands of little frogs hopping through the grass. Cyril reckoned that they were from the tadpoles that filled the pond in the Verclut quarry, not a few hundred yards away. They had disappeared by the next day when I wanted to photograph the unusual phenomenon. On another occasion I had the job of leading the old grey mare as it pulled the harvester in a field of oats that we were cutting just inland from the Seymour Inn. We would then have to trim the inaccessible corners with a sickle and bind each stook by hand. Not knowing much about those large, four legged animals I didn't realise that, when turning at the end of a row they lifted one front hoof over the other. Too late, I lifted my foot out of the way and one very heavy horse's hoof crashed on to my gumboot crushing it into the, fortunately, now dry, soft soil. Did it hurt! No bones broken, but, being the youngest, as usual I was the butt of all humour on the farm. To complete my misfortune on this particular day, when I wasn't looking, they filled my jacket pockets with dried horse manure which I didn't discover until I had arrived back at the Exeter that evening.

Late in the season there was a bit of a disaster. As it was a wet beginning to September the grain stooks that hadn't been gathered in were dampened by rain and in a few days were sprouting green at the tops and ruined.

The two brothers were great mates, patient and helpful to me and always worked hard. They had one very unusual trait to my mind. They had very bad and fragile tempers. One word out of place and I would turn to find them both on the ground fighting like furies. This happened frequently, but it always turned out to be peaceful in the end, both working together as if nothing had happened. I am glad I never tangled with them as they were strong and very tough. I never saw them again after leaving the farm in the September.

At the end of the war, Don joined his father Mike Le Clercq, a La Rocque fisherman, and they fished together for lobster, prawns, spider crab and mackerel, all when in season. Mike and Don were well liked La Rocque fishermen. Unfortunately, in 1948 when returning to La Rocque Harbour from the outlying Goubiniere reef in their boat, the Daddy, they were caught in a violent thunder storm while in a patch of open water. Suddenly, when beneath a heavy cloud, lightning struck the anchor in the bow killing Don instantaneously and leaving Mike, deeply shocked, to bring his dead son, badly burned, back into La Rocque Harbour. There was a history of tragedy in this family of La Rocque fishermen. A generation past, Mike's father, also a La Rocque fisherman was also lost at sea in their boat, the Pelican, when it was returning from the Minquier reefs in a gale after the usual week's fishing for lobster and prawns around the islets. This was told me by Edmund, another brother who fished with Mike after Don's death and who was still fishing there in the Daddy, when I joined them with my boat from 1976 until 1982. Edmund also had a rather sensitive temper which I discovered on occasions to my cost, but he was still a great friend and helped me as much as possible with my fishing endeavours.

As that summer season came to an end I was able to fulfil my wish for a better camera. In Mulcaster Street, opposite to Dalys Hotel, the Bunch of Grapes, there was a combined tobacconist and camera shop owned by a Mr Christin. He became quite a friend and helped me to obtain chemicals and photographic papers now in short supply. The Germans had supplied him with an allocation of cameras to sell to the Forces. He didn't have to account for each camera as they were forbidden to the civilian population, but he was good enough to take a chance and sell me a Carl Zeiss Nettar folding one/twenty for the sum of three pounds ten shillings (£3.50). Strangely enough I never had better results than from my Kodak Box Brownie although it was much easier to keep hidden. Mr Christin had a legitimate photographic business and developed and printed black and white photographs from a dark room behind the shop counter, and from which he could see anyone entering the shop without being seen. One day, possibly in a rash moment, he showed me a wonderful collection of prints copied from negatives brought in by the soldiers and sailors. There were superb photographs of aircraft at the Airport, gun emplacements, shipping in the Harbour, of visiting film stars and notabilities, all of excellent quality. They would have been of great interest and value after the war. Unfortunately, during a scare, possibly when I was imprisoned in September 1942, he wisely, if sadly, burned the lot. Most of my photographs went the same way, the family destroying them quickly every time the Exeter was searched by the Feldgendarmerie as they would have got me into even more trouble.

The Germans frequently had manoeuvres either in the countryside or occasionally in the town. I often wished that I had been able to obtain a miniature camera to record these activities. On one occasion in particular I was cycling up St Clement's Road during this training exercise with fully-armed soldiers rushing around on exercises. Suddenly, racing up the road towards the Ritz Hotel, Colomberie, came a pale blue MGTC sports car with a German steel-helmeted private at the wheel and beside him a young, rather dapper officer with a machine gun, the stand resting on the bonnet. What a picture it would have made! He was obviously having a marvellous day out in his personal commandeered non-armoured car!

In the autumn of 1941 the family decided to rent a bungalow in Pontorson Lane in St Clements. My mother had always wanted to move away from the pub and live in the country and we were able to rent this furnished property, a bungalow by the name of 'Suncote' which had been evacuated by its occupants in June 1940. It had a large garden in which we hoped to grow vegetables and I was able to buy a sectional chicken house from George D. Laurens hoping to obtain a supply of eggs which had become in very short supply. This proved to be a bit of a disaster as the chickens produced few eggs as I couldn't obtain the correct poultry food. As well as vegetables, my dad, a heavy smoker, had other things in mind and soon obtained a supply of tobacco plants. The growing of these was a success and in a short time we were drying and curing the huge leaves in the garage. He said that the tobacco produced was not wonderful but seemed to satisfy some sort of craving.

While living at 'Suncote' we had a cross-bred German Alsatian by the name of Rex as a guard dog. For most of the time he was well behaved, but on occasions, when German soldiers ran along the lane on exercises he would bark and attack them, their uniforms possibly being the cause. The soldiers strangely enough seemed to be fond of all animals and never retaliated.

During the summer months the Germans had frequent band concerts in the Royal Square. Some civilians, as well as soldiers, would hang around to listen and on several occasions one of the town's eccentrics, one George Le Sueur, would mock the German band with strange antics and also by doing a hornpipe to the music. George was a powerfully built, rather stocky individual with staring pale blue eyes and a shock of curly grey hair. However, the Germans soon found out that George's behaviour was caused by him being shell-shocked in the First World War, were very tolerant of his behaviour and had him led quietly away from the Square. We knew George quite well as there was a very amusing story about his strange behaviour a year or two before the war. He was known to be a very good painter and decorator. At the time he was working for Houillebecqs, the firm that carried out all of Ann Street Brewery's work on their many pubs. On this occasion he was working on our first floor at the Exeter with a blow-lamp. Suddenly, the lamp burst into flames and George, with great presence of mind immediately grabbed the nearest piece of cloth which turned out to be Mr Houillebecq's good jacket, rolled it around the blow lamp and flung it out of the open window on to Queen Street below. Mr Houillebecq was not amused.

It was at the end of 1941 that the Germans commenced the building of reinforced concrete gun emplacements and camouflaged personnel huts on the same Verclut headland where I had been working during the summer months. They installed on this headland an infantry strongpoint with reinforced bunkers which commanded a view of the coast from Gorey nearly as far as Green Island. It was in the spring of 1942 that I was made aware of an artillery battery. I had read in the Monday edition of the Evening Post a notice to the effect that on the following day there would be "Scharfschiessen" (Sharpshooting) to take place on the south coast and low-water fishermen should stay well clear. That afternoon, I ambled to the beach from our bungalow, wondering whether to go further down and hunt out some crabs. Suddenly, there was a distant booming sound and then a whistling, whirring noise, seemingly overhead and then the loud crashing of exploding shells in the area of Icho Tower. These had come from a 10cm battery of field guns which had been emplaced in La Rue au Blanc facing St Clement's Bay. One would have thought that it would have been possible to see these shells passing overhead, but as sound travels much slower than light, by the time one heard the noise, they were well past. In August 1944 eight 15cm guns were transferred from Guernsey and four of them were emplaced at Verclut. From this position they could command a view of their targets from Gorey Castle right around the south-east coast. On one occasion a shell scored a direct hit on the side of Icho Tower. Later in the year I took particular notice as to where the shell had struck but the only sign of damage was a slight gouging out of the exterior granite wall which was many feet thick. This artillery practice continued throughout the Occupation and on one occasion, whilst swimming at Havre des Pas pool, there was a line of explosions between the Demi des Pas lighthouse and the Dog's Nest. Masses of rocks, gravel, sand and seaweed hurtled into the air when the shells struck, the firing possibly coming from the guns at Fort Regent.

We had no football field at the Beeches and every week we would cycle to the F. B. Fields for training. On one morning in February our class cycled down as usual and were the first team out practising. By the time our training was over all other pitches were occupied. Returning to the dressing rooms to change we discovered that all the other pitches were occupied by German soldiers as their uniforms were everywhere to be seen. Hanging on two of the pegs were two fine Luger .38 automatic pistols. More souvenirs! Without further thought, Pat and I each grabbed one, hid them into our training gear and off we went. Unfortunately, it didn't end there.

Next morning, the class was paraded in front of the school house as a German officer arrived with a Jersey policeman, P.C. Le Gentil. He told the class and a glowering Brother Edward that two pistols had been taken from the changing rooms at the F.B. Fields and that he wanted them back, and that there would be no punishment if this was done. A bit later Pat and I agreed that we had no option but to return the guns as the whole team knew what we had done, so I collected them from a school pal, John Green, who had offered to hide them in his father's front room cabinet. His father was assistant manager at Barclays Bank. I think he would have had a blue fit if he had known what was hidden in his front room! As there was no point in both of us getting into trouble, and as it was my idea, I said that I would return the pistols to Feldgendarmerie headquarters at Tudor House near where we had pinched the road signs. That afternoon, with shaking knees, I knocked on the door to be admitted by the same German officer. I was given a gentle scolding, told not to be so stupid again and having taken my particulars, told me that nothing more would be done. Unfortunately, Brother Edward didn't take the same lenient attitude and Pat and I were quite sore for the few days to follow.

Early in 1942 one of the French skippers of a barge which used to operate between St Malo and St Helier approached my dad in the bar, and asked him if he would like to buy some black market brandy. When my father asked him how many bottles, he replied, "Not bottles, Reg, I have two barrels on board if you would like to buy them." My dad, quite shaken at the offer, said that it would be impossible to get them past the guards on the North Quay so there was nothing doing. He said this without realising that his pal and customer, one Mc

Clusky, an Irish truck driver was listening. Like most other Irishmen living in the Island at the time he had no option but to work for the occupying forces to earn a wage. For employment he had to drive for the Germans and being neutral wasn't breaking the law. It was, either work for them or starve. He then said, "No problem, Reg , I have an official pass for the harbours and they know me well, I'll get them off for you." And so the deal was done. The next day Mac collected the barrels from the barge on the North Quay, covered them with sacks and drove off the quay without any problems, showing his Harbour pass to the duty soldiers who knew him well. He then stopped and picked up my dad and his bike outside the Great Western pub where he had been waiting anxiously. Dad had told the French skipper that he would pay after he had sampled the contents of each barrel. He had heard many stories of bottles of brandy or whisky being sold, the contents being substituted with cold tea!

To commence with, the plan went without a hitch and he and his bike were picked up as planned outside the pub. Mc Clusky, cool as a cucumber, my dad shaking in his shoes, drove over Mount Bingham and along the coast road until they arrived at Millard's Corner. There, to my dad's horror, the German truck ran out of fuel. He was nearly passing out, Mc Clusky calmly alighted and went into the billet next to the German bunker and explained to the N.C.O. on duty what had happened. He showed the soldier his pass and signed for a full jerrycan which he promptly emptied in to the tank and returned the can. They then drove on to Pontorson Lane and to "Suncote" where the barrels were placed on to a ramp and tapped by my dad. The contents proved to be genuine and that night the skipper was paid. During the next few months the brandy was individually bottled, then sold or bartered for tea, pork, sugar beet and other commodities which had become very scarce. The amount of goods that had fallen off the back of Irish driven

German Army trucks, to quote a phrase, was considerable, and we saw quite a lot of it.

The back of the ground floor of our pub, alongside of the gents' toilet was a vertical tunnel, bounded by Edna's bakery on the right and the property on the left. Its only access to this gap was by a small window, just large enough for a person to crawl through. Edna's bakery had closed before the war and the property was vacant when the Germans had arrived. Sometime later they requisitioned it as a store for domestic articles.

There was also a German or Austrian civilian caretaker who dwelt on the premises. He wore Austrian type garments and had a sporting rifle with a telescopic sight and would often go into the country, returning with a bag of rabbits or woodpigeons. He never spoke to us or even acknowledged my father. The building was full of kitchen utensils, brushes, electric light bulbs and a large variety of other domestic commodities like catering saucepans and boilers. I knew of these things because, one afternoon when he left on one of his forays, I climbed on to our roof, on to his and through a skylight in to the premises looking for souvenirs, but without luck. I helped myself to a few articles that I thought might be of use and took them back to my dad. He was furious, told me that they didn't belong to us, I would get into more trouble and to take them back, telling me that when the war was over maybe I could make another attempt. I bore that in mind, returned the articles as I had that sporting rifle in my sights and thought that it would make a good souvenir when the Occupation had come to an end.

One afternoon McClusky and another Irish driver stopped their truck outside the Exeter to deliver more goods to the store. They both went in but McClusky stayed longer and as they were driving off Mac had a quick word with my puzzled dad saying that he would be in to see him after work. Just before we opened for a spell at 6pm, Mac arrived outside with his truck, grinned at my dad, walked past him as if going to the gents' toilet, slithered through the small window and pushed several sacks of goods on to our premises. They had been dropped down the vertical tunnel from the next door attic when the Austrian caretaker wasn't looking. He quickly loaded the gear on to his lorry and drove off to return a little later with a couple of bottles for my dad as a thank you. Mac was a quiet individual, about five foot eight and well built. He was famous amongst his mates for an episode which made him quite a hero. On a previous occasion a crowd of civilians in Broad Street were watching a group of Organization Todt slave workers being marched through the streets to some destination in the country. It was a pitiful sight as they were dressed in rags and a murmuring crowd were being pushed back by a few soldiers off duty at the time. One had the misfortune to give our irate Mac a shove. Before he knew what was happening the German soldier was on his back nursing a sore jaw and the Irishman had disappeared into the crowd. The German hadn't realised that many Irishmen had short fuses to his cost.

It was now early in 1942. Boredom, restrictions, shortage of food and lack of activities were having an effect on the Island's youth and some from Victoria College and the Beeches were becoming troublesome to the German police and occupying cells in the town prison in Gloucester Street. I remember two from our class were particularly venturesome, spying out German stores during the day and dodging the patrols after curfew to steal food and equipment, mostly for the devil of it all. Donald Bell and Dickie Williams were the most daring, we all knew about their activities as they often produced some of their booty at school the next day and at one time most of the fifth form at The Beeches were wearing German dispatch rider's gauntlets, green and identifiable from normal mitts as they had a trigger finger! On occasions Brother Edward, the Head, would become furious and frustrated as quite a few members of his form were residing in the local prison in Gloucester Street!

One day, brother-in law Frank Crowhurst turned up when my dad wasn't present and gave me a parcel. Grinning rather irresponsibly he watched me unwrap the object from its sacking cover. It was a beautiful German officer's 9mm Mauser automatic pistol, leather holster and clip of ammunition. He knew that I had been trying to get hold of one. He had picked it up from an unwary officer's desk at the harbours where he was working as a crane driver. I took it home to Pontorson Lane, oiled it well and hid it in the interior of our wooden gramophone, there to lie undetected for the time being. Later I hid it on a shelf under the chicken house until I gave it back to Frank to look after in safety after my spell in jail in September 1942.

Havre des Pas swimming pool was our gathering place during the spring, summer and autumn seasons. There were swimming competitions and water-polo matches but none of these activities included any members of the occupying forces as it was considered unpatriotic to fraternise with these troops even when they were off duty. On one or two occasions groups of soldiers marched into the pool premises for swimming lessons. We sat back with interest especially when the sergeant insisted that each man do a backward dead drop from the ten foot diving board. He made no exception for those who couldn't swim except for tying a short rope around the waist of the frightened trooper to pull the unfortunate man out of the water by the rope, spluttering and half drowned when he came to the surface. As they were Germans we thought that this was great fun but made sure that the sergeant didn't see us laughing at their plight.

On another occasion a troop of soldiers marched on to the pool premises in full uniform, rifles and steel helmets, after a route march in hot summer weather. They sat together resting on the highest viewing benches just behind the diving boards, laughing and obviously enjoying some sort of joke. Suddenly, one of them, possibly for a bet, got up, lay down his rifle, helmet and other equipment, climbed on to the top diving board and dived fully clothed into the pool! He quickly returned to his mates, collected his winnings, retrieved his rifle etc. and they marched off hoping that the episode hadn't been observed by their N.C.O.

I have to admit that never in those five years of visiting the pool did they ever interfere with any of our activities, neither did they try to chat up any of the girls in our group. Possibly they had too many volunteers in the town!

Single .... Single. Married, Widow or Widower
(Ledig, Verheiratet, Verwitwet)

Dark .... Colour of Hair
(Farbe des Haares)

Brown .... Colour of Eyes
(Farbe der Augen)

None ....
.... Physical Peculiarities
(Besondere Merkmale)

Kevin John Le Cocq .... Signature
(Unterschrift)

Holder   *Kevin John Le Cocq*
(Inhaber)

Residing at   *22 Queen Street*
(Wohnhaft)   *St Helier Jersey*

Born on the *3rd Dec:* at *St Helier*
(Geboren am) *1926* (in) *Jersey*

Registration Officer.
(Das Meldeamt).

Kevin's second ID card
issued 14th January 1941
and Occupation Reichmarks
issued by the Germans for
the occupied territories

Above: A posed photograph of officers of Machine Gun Battalion 16

On parade. A company from Infantry Regiment 582 form a Guard of Honour to greet Field Marshal von Witzleben on 11th July 1941

Above is another photograph taken by Kevin of troops marching up Queen street in front of Boot's the chemist. It was taken from an upstairs room in the Exeter Hotel.

Full military honours.The Funeral of two RAF pilots shot down over Jersey in June 1943. Two lorry loads of wreaths were sent by Jersey residents

Friendly Faces. A staged propaganda photo showing that the troops had been "accepted" by the Islanders

Kevin on "Stroppy". Summer 1941

A New Occupation, But Different

In 1942, as many pupils from Victoria College and De La Salle were getting into trouble with the German authorities, some public spirited members of the Societe Jersiaise decided to form junior groups in order to keep us schoolboys out of trouble. At the end of April they organised a meeting at the Museum which was attended by Pat McGarry and Ron Smith from De La Salle and quite a few from Victoria College and the Girls' College. Our pair attended to see how interesting it might be but I didn't bother to go. The first bird watching meeting was to be in Queen's Valley the following Sunday. I wasn't particularly interested until they mentioned that a crowd of Girls' College students, some of them quite attractive, would be going along so I decided to join them. Roderick Dobson, our ornithologist group leader led the way down the valley pointing out nests of various birds - robins, blackbirds, chiff-chaffs and many other common birds that we didn't even know existed, and a particular rarity, a nesting grey wagtail. We four were at the tail end of the group and when no one was watching we individually helped ourselves to one egg from each nest just enjoying the mischief of the situation. Roderick was highly amused when told about this episode later in the summer when just a few of us remained in the group and became keen and avid birdwatchers.

Throughout the summer of 1942 our group would accompany Rod Dobson to various parts of the Island, to areas of cliff not mined by the Germans. We explored the valleys and south-east shoreline, not just learning about the various species of bird, but becoming familiar with parts of the Island that we had never heard of before. We were taught the names of the various gullies on the north coast and shown the nests of peregrine falcons and ravens. Queen's Valley was of particular interest as the eastern slope was fortified with big roll-bombs (ex French artillery shells) wired to the trees and ready to destroy any allied tanks should they venture up the valley. We made sure to keep well clear of them. From the lower end of the valley we saw hundreds of slave workers on the Grouville Bay shoreline, building the concrete fortifications and anti-tank wall where the bungalows used to be. However, on that first May outing, forty seven of us marched down Queens's Valley, driving all before us and, as Roderick said later, "It wasn't the most successful of outings." However, I found bird watching a riveting occupation, and have stayed a keen observer of our feathered friends from that time, which saved me from further problems with the occupying authorities, at least, for the time being.

In March and April 1942, when the family had moved back to the Exeter, two pals from school with a mate would come in during the evenings to play cards. They were Peter Hassell and Denis Audrain with their older friend Maurice Gould. Maurice, I believe, was the nephew of the Australian herbalist whose shop was just around the corner, but who wouldn't have cards played on the premises. We would play pontoon and skylark around but when I left the room they seemed to be whispering about some sort of secret. I was to find out this mystery suddenly on May 3rd. The news came out that on the previous night three boys had tried to escape by boat from Green Island. Their boat had sunk and Denis Audrain, unable to swim, drowned and the other two were captured. The trio had no idea of navigation or the sea or rocks around Green Island. They started the outboard motor on full throttle, the boat shot off at speed in a circle, struck a rock and disintegrated. Denis's body was recovered and Peter Hassell and Maurice Gould were found the following morning, roughed up, interrogated, tried and deported to be imprisoned on the Continent. Maurice died of T.B. many months later, but Peter, a really tough individual, survived the war and I met him once again, many years later. They really kept a good secret as I hadn't a clue as to what they were up to before being told about the tragedy.

A Peaceful Time

One day in June news got around that good catches of mackerel were being caught on the east coast especially at Archirondel and St Catherine's. Our entire crowd had made up rods with long bamboo poles from that wonderful emporium of George D. Laurens, the hardware store of Queen Street which sold everything from tin-tacks and rolls of barbed wire to suites of furniture. The two men, who managed the hardware department, one a Mr Le Vesconte, if my memory serves me right, were most helpful, cut the poles and joined the pieces with brass ferrules fixed with plaster and glue, the eyes taped with string with a fastening around the base for the wooden reel.

Pat Smut, Nev Le Boutillier, Terry Stuart and I set out one sunny morning to see if we could catch a few mackerel for the table. We tried off the rocks at Archirondel to commence with but without much luck. The only thing hooked was Pat Mc Garry's ear when Nev made a bad cast. Pat was not amused but we thought that it was great fun and hoped that his ear wasn't the only thing we were going to catch on that lovely June day. From the rocks at the Tower we proceeded to the end of the breakwater and although the sea was alive with whitebait and sand eels being chased by mackerel we had no luck. Six p.m. was approaching and we had to be out of the military zone at the base of the breakwater by that time. We packed up the rods and gear and cycled back to find the sea at the slipway swarming with mackerel. Out with the gear again and in no time we all had a reasonable catch, my bag being eighteen. Unfortunately they were horse mackerel or scad, not a good eating fish but in those hard times any sort of food was acceptable.

It was now dusk so we split up, rushing back to town on our cycles, hoping to be in before curfew. I was alone and it was dark by the time that I had arrived at St Saviour's Parish Hall. I hurtled down the hill to be brought to an abrupt halt at the bottom by the shining light of the German patrol's sergeant's torch. There were four of them, one N.C.O. with a sub-machine gun and three armed privates. It was about ten minutes past curfew and the sergeant pointed to his watch with the comment, "Sie sind spat, warum ?" I knew what he meant and pointed to my fishing creel. He looked inside and said, "Wo wohnen sie?" Showing off the little German that I knew, I replied, "In Koenig Strasse in der Stadt."and gave him my identity card to examine. The sergeant grinned, clipped me around the ear and said, "Gehen sie snell zu hause" or words to that effect and I was off in a flash. My dad was waiting on the doorstep of the Exeter, worried as usual but a bit pacified at the sight of the fish. We had them the next day, not good eating but by then any food was welcome.

The spring and summer of 1942 was spent with pal Jimmy and a few friends from Victoria College who used to meet on the promenade alongside of Dr Mattas' house, "Craig Tara", at La Mare. We would surf on the big tides in the evenings and at low water we would paddle out to a rock called La Sambue to swim in the crystal clear water and potter around the rocks looking for the very abundant octopus and other marine life. On one occasion, after a summer gale a barge had been wrecked off the Demi des Pas lighthouse and wreckage was coming up along the tide line. Jim and I arrived late and the gang pointed out a barrel that had been washed up on the tide line a few hundred yards away and suggested we go and have a look. We should have known. Half way to our objective there was the crack of a rifle being fired and the bullet whined over our heads. The Germans had placed guards along the coast to stop the locals from beachcombing.

Just a warning and a great joke to the gang who had already been warned off hunting for wreckage.

As the summer turned to autumn we began meeting in Hugh La Cloche's grandmother's garage in Hastings Lane. The College boys had got hold of some ether and would muck about putting each other out cold for the fun of it and sticking needles into each of the unconscious 'victims' to prove that the ether was working! This wasn't for Jimmy or me but we did have a great deal of excitement practising on a target on the inner door of the garage with our 9mm pistols. Hugh had purchased a Polish Radom automatic 9mm pistol from Peter Hassel for five pounds the previous winter and we wished to try his pistol and my Mauser at a target in the garage. We put layer upon layer of wood and a target on the inner door and each took turns to fire. It really was quite stupid as the headquarters and offices of the Island Commandant were at the Hotel Metropole in Roseville Street, not a hundred yards away! The other shock came when the inner garage door was examined from the outside as huge splinters had been ripped out of the pristine woodwork and Hugh had to explain to the family how this had come about when we finally got out of jail at the beginning of October.

In mid-September orders were published in the Evening Post to the effect that all English born residents were to be deported to Germany. This came as a great shock, not only to the Islanders but also to the German authorities as the orders had come directly from German headquarters in Berlin. However, as this order had come from Hitler himself, even though protests were made, the German Führer was adamant. These people had to go, regardless of age or health. The reasons given were that the British authorities in Persia (now Iran) had interned all German civilians as there was a great deal of spying activities carried out by these residents. The Nazi leader was furious and determined to get his revenge.

The first group of deportees had left on September 16th. On September 18th, another exodus took place, the ship leaving with four hundred and thirty-six persons on board. There were anti-German demonstrations by civilians at the Weighbridge with the crowd moving to Pier Road overlooking the Harbour, shouting and singing patriotic songs to encourage the deportees.We were surprised and a bit disgusted that our local government officials were not making a more vociferous protest at the deporting of these English residents who were obviously suffering at the thought of being sent in cargo boats to an unknown destination and fate in the middle of the war. Apart from other demonstrations on September 16th and 18th, the time of the first deportation, I am ashamed to say that our illegal gathering at South Hill on September 29th, was the only outward demonstration of anger against the German occupiers during the five Occupation years, and that was by a crowd of disorganised youngsters.

On September 29th the third group were to be deported, so our gang decided to visit South Hill, where overlooking the pier heads, we could shout and cheer them on their way. Leaving our cycles at Hugh's grandmother's garage in Hastings Lane, six or eight of us walked along Havre des Pas and up Mount Bingham. By this time we realised that many others from the town had the same idea in mind. By the time we had reached the cliffs at South Hill there was quite a gathering of youths heading for the Harbour. Above us, on the cliff-top, a German sentry was guarding the four barrelled 20mm "Vierling" anti-aircraft gun. He was in a great coat, as it was a cool autumn evening, steel helmet and rifle slung over his shoulder. He was looking down with interest at this unusual and forbidden gathering of about forty plus noisy youths. We soon reached the low wall overlooking the old lifeboat shed and by then about twenty more young people had arrived from Pier Road. We were soon shouting and jostling around in a disorderly manner.

Suddenly, an older man arrived with a bicycle, basket on the front containing a little dog. He was a local by the name of Barbier, Marcel I think. He placed the cycle against the wall and turned to the crowd. "Come on lads, let's give them a good send off" and proceeded to lead us in patriotic songs, the first one being "There will always be an England" and followed by other songs that we had been forbidden to sing for the previous two years. By this time we couldn't care less about German orders as we were really hyped up and absolutely bored and fed up by the mass of German soldiers now occupying the Island.

After a short while there was a muffled explosion from the new tunnel beneath, possibly set off to frighten us away. It had no effect and we continued singing and shouting. A yell from one of our crowd quickly brought us to our senses. We looked over the wall to see a squad of about thirty German soldiers on bicycles, rifles over their shoulders and pedalling furiously in our direction, turning at the Harvey Memorial and heading towards our crowd. We continued singing until they arrived. They then dismounted, threw their cycles against the wall, formed a line, rifles across their chests and moved towards us, roughly shoving us back.

The young under-officer, who was in charge was very excited by now and was shouting at us, "Raus, raus, go home or you will be in trouble." Truculently we moved back, pushed by these soldiers, holding their rifles across their chests, some towards Mount Bingham, our crowd along Pier Road until we moved into Mulcaster Street.

Here, there were people out for the evening by now, soldiers with their Jersey girl friends enjoying their evening strolls and, as we were still excited after the fracas at South Hill, we shouted obscenities at them to their great annoyance. They screamed back at us but the soldiers were more amused than angry and continued arm in arm with their welcoming friends. We moved across the Weighbridge and along the Esplanade, hoping to see something of interest from the Harbour but all was now quiet. Since the last disturbance at Pier Road, curfew had been changed from eleven to ten o'clock. As it was now getting late we decided to return to Hastings Lane, ambling quietly up Kensington Place and down The Parade. All seemed uneventful, that is until I reached the corner of Gloucester Street and General Don's statue.

It was now dusk and time to be home. Suddenly I received a heavy thump across my shoulders which nearly knocked me off of my feet and two burly pairs of hands grabbed me and I was clouted and frog-marched back up The Parade. We then turned into Kensington Place and I was thrown into the foyer of the Barra House Hotel, which was now a German army billet. We were made to stand against the wall, hands above our heads and struck with a rifle butt whenever we turned to see what else was going on in the room. There was a constant clatter of jack-boots on the wood floor, which was a good job as, I am sure that they would have heard the knocking of my frightened knees! We must have been there for over an hour and when I was given permission to go to the toilet I was able to tear out some incriminating pages from my pocket diary and flush them away. Suddenly the Field Police arrived, under the command of a particularly evil looking sergeant, whose face we knew well. They were in steel helmets, great coats, chain and insignia around their necks. I was scared, wondering what I had got myself into. I was certainly no heroic member of the Resistance!

We were lined up, all fourteen of us, in twos. We were searched, our identity cards taken. Hugh La Cloche was knocked down when the sergeant found an empty 9mm cartridge case in a little pouch on his belt. On the orders of the sergeant, six soldiers made a show of loading up their rifles, three on each side of our column. We were then warned that if we took one step out of place we would be shot. Five minutes later we left the hotel and were then marched in the dark, up Kensington Place, down The Parade, into Gloucester Street and to the prison where the guards were waiting to let us in. We were led up to cells on the first floor on the civilian wing, four to a cell. Hugh La Cloche, Doug Liron, Dave Bartlett and I shared one cell. This had four low wooden beds, straw mattresses, one pillow and army blankets. We were obviously worried and it was some time before we were able to sleep and I just wondered what sort of trouble I had got myself in to. There was a commotion later that night and the next day we were told that the Germans had brought Barbier in, having roughed him up quite badly during interrogation but we didn't see him as he was placed in the German section.

We fourteen were roused sharply at seven, nothing to eat or drink, rushed down to the courtyard, and bundled into small vans to be driven to Feldgendarmerie Headquarters at the same mock Tudor house on the corner of Bagatelle Road and Claremont Road. We were interrogated in twos for several hours by officers who spoke fluent English. I was paired with a country lad by the name of Bridou. I am sure he had nothing to do with our disturbance but was just caught up in the melée on the previous evening. Our details were taken by the officer and my misdemeanour with the stolen pistols was mentioned. As well as my identity card, my small pocket diary was open on his desk, and he was quite annoyed with me as I alluded to the soldiers as Huns, an expression that they disliked intensely.

A month or two before, Pat McGarry, Ron Smith and I had made a trip out to the north coast to a gully called Le Creux Gabourel where Rod Dobson had shown us a hole in the cliff where a kestrel falcon was nesting. I wanted a young one as a pet so, one day, Pat climbed down to the nesting hole with a rope and extricated a nearly fledged youngster for me to take home. For several weeks I kept her in a cage on our lead roof, feeding her on insects and mice which I had caught in traps. Soon she became too difficult to keep, and the final straw for the family came when she escaped, flew around the top floor of the Exeter, our home, finally landing on the mirror of my grandmother's dressing table. This nearly caused her to have a heart attack, the sight of this fierce little falcon staring at her intently when she entered her bedroom! A few days later, on instructions from the family, I took my pet to the north coast, released her and she flew strongly away.

The German officer was particularly interested in my notes on the bird, wanting to know if this species of falcon attacked pigeons. He was persistent, wanting to know details as to why I should want to keep one. What was its food, and would it attack homing pigeons? I could see where this was leading and it took a long time to convince him that this small predator was smaller than a pigeon and lived on mice and beetles which it captured by hovering above its prey. In the end, he seemed to accept my explanation.

Poor old Bridou came next. Ruddy faced, beret pulled tightly over his head and still in his gumboots, it was obvious that he was even more scared than I was. Examining his papers, the officer looked up and said, "Herr Bridou, I see that you have been working for us."

Bridou brightened visibly. "Yes Sir, I was." Then, glancing up sternly he looked angrily at poor Bridou and said, "Then,Vi are you not vorking for us now?" Scared though I was, I had to grin. Poor Bridou sank visibly into his chair, speechless and was then, to his relief, told to go and sit down. We were there until about four, and then driven back in the same vans to our cells in Gloucester Street and were, by this time, very hungry!

September 1942.
A young Kevin with his Kestrel Falcon that caused
concern to an interrogating German police officer.

Two weeks in Gloucester Street

When I hadn't arrived home the previous night my worried father phoned Jersey police headquarters to find out any news. He spoke to a friend, Sergeant Tom Cross who told him that there had been trouble in the town and that the Germans had locked up a crowd of schoolboys for the night for creating a disturbance. We were then living at Pontorson Lane at the time and in the morning, straight after curfew was lifted, he rushed in to the Exeter on his bike, borrowed the handcart from Orviss the fish shop, as the Germans were already checking the house numbers in Queen Street, beginning at Snow Hill. He then quickly moved our radio and one or two other forbidden articles from the pub before their arrival. The place was searched, nothing untoward was found as they didn't realise that we were now living in the country. My gun and other forbidden articles were not discovered. It was the same with Hugh as his gun was hidden in his Gran's garage. They saw my British Army first aid box, paid it little attention after examining the contents, and then moved out.

There were fourteen of us imprisoned that night. In our cell were Hugh La Cloche, Doug Liron and Dave Bartlett from Victoria College and myself from the Beeches. In another cell were three Irishmen and poor old Bridou and, if my memory serves me right, there were three boys of a similar age, one Kenny Matthews, Doug Buesnel and Dennis Le Cuirot, who, in the July of 1944 had the temerity to join a crowd of foreign workers who were being transported back to France, and later, after many dangerous escapades, managed to join the Allied forces in Normandy.

On one occasion we had to scrub out our cells and we each took it in turns to do our quarter. Poor Bridou. The Irishmen just sat back and made him scrub out the whole room! Of the others, I can't remember. That evening the Germans gave permission for food to be brought in to us in the prison. Most people sent in sandwiches or similar snacks. Not my dad! He rushed into Joe Blake's the butcher, next door to the Exeter, scrounged some steak, fried it with onions and chips, plated it with another plate for cover and, on his bike, raced hurriedly down to the prison with my supper. Imagine the nostrils of the German and local warders when the smell of fried onions with steak and chips wafted across their noses after two years of rationing. Reluctantly we were given the food but not knives and forks so shared out the chips and onions with our fingers and took it in turns to have bites out of the piece of steak! That was the last food permitted to be brought in to the prison. For the next fortnight we had to live on the usual prison fare. I think that I lost about seven pounds in those two weeks.

Next day we were told by the Jersey warders that we were lucky to be in the debtors' cells and that they were more comfortable than the others. These were more luxurious, which didn't say much for the normal cells. They were whitewashed and had a small Victorian fireplace and mantelpiece in one corner. There was also a large metal pipe running down the outside wall, which we presumed was for room heating in winter. It was to prove of great use a few days later. There was also a high barred window which could be reached, if standing on one another's shoulders

Our breakfast consisted of a small chunk of coarse brown bread, a small piece of butter or margarine, and a chipped enamel mug of unsweetened black ersatz coffee. For our main mid-day meal we had a large chipped enamel mug of half rotten potatoes in their skins and a large chipped enamel mug of watery, tasteless cabbage soup with a suspicion of meat but devoid of salt and no bread. On the second day, Doug Liron lifted out a piece of cow or horse jawbone with several rotten teeth still attached. He placed it on the mantelpiece as a souvenir but a warder must have removed it that day when we were exercising. For tea we were given another small chunk of husky brown bread, a small piece of margarine and on every other day a small morsel of jam. We were always hungry and spent most evenings and nights chatting about food, that is, until governor Briard sent a warder up to tell us to keep quiet.

On the second day we were marched down in fours to the ablutions. This consisted of a large wooden tub with the water heated in a huge copper in the corner. To my horror, we were told to strip, given a piece of coarse soap and told to get in. A quick scrub, out, dried and then given a short hair cut. I was a bit shy and not used to prison discipline especially, stripping in front of a crowd of men! Then back to the cells. Each morning and afternoon we had thirty minutes exercise. There were other Jersey men who had been imprisoned without trial for several weeks, two of them, decorators, had been caught stealing petrol, a serious crime to the occupying authorities. One whispered to me that he was starving so I decided to keep the potatoes, that I couldn't face, for him and on the next exercise period I sneaked them to him in a coloured piece of cloth. I was caught by one of the Jersey warders by the name of Paine, given a dressing down and sent back to my cell with a flea in my ear! During that fortnight we considered that we were treated poorly by the Jersey warders as if we were criminals and not political prisoners. There was another by the name of Ozouf who made it his business to make life as difficult as possible. We hated him as well as the governor, Briard, who was always fawning to his German masters.

The Dickensian Jail

Our cells were locked for the night at six and we were told to make sure that we visited the toilet before that time. After two or three days I had occasion to pay a call to that gaunt edifice at the end of the corridor, just before closing time at six. The walls were of cold dark granite, ceilings that high that one could hardly see them. I was sitting in quiet contemplation considering my fate and still afraid of what might happen to us when I noticed that there was no toilet paper as such, only a thick wad of old newspaper wired to a nail in the wall. The paper was yellowed with age and the print old fashioned. With nothing better to do I tore off the first sheet to read. To my amazement it was part of the front page of a London newspaper, but it was the heading that stood out in large letters that startled me. "The Daily News, Editor Charles Dickens," the date, January 1846. In this grave predicament I was so surprised and shocked that I forgot to keep it. To think that I was incarcerated in this Dickensian prison, reading a newspaper edited by Charles Dickens! Where had these newspapers been for nearly one hundred years? In which town attic or cellar had they been stored and forgotten? For many days after I hunted for more gems but without success.

Two days after our arrival we were lying on our beds reading the few available books when we heard a tapping from the metal pipe along the wall. Hugh got down and putting his ear to the pipe he tapped back. He then heard a voice transmitted along the metal and began a conversation with the occupants a few cells away. They were a Mr and Mrs Ross. He was my dentist and he and his wife were imprisoned for feeding and giving the news to the unfortunate Russian slave workers who were building the Island's fortifications.

The Ross's were caught, tried, sentenced to six months in jail and transported to France. They were not able to get back to the Island until after the Liberation. When they returned they had lost a great deal of weight and were suffering from their ordeal of imprisonment in France. They were a wonderful inspiration to us, never thinking of themselves, just encouraging us to be brave and not to worry too much.

I think that their heroism was not acknowledged by the Russian Embassy after the war, either because the Russians were not told about the Ross's activities or because they were not members of the Communist Party. This is, of course, just my interpretation as to what had happened.

Nothing seemed to occur for the next two weeks. We were given a few old books to read but were permanently bored, hungry and frustrated with no idea how long we would be inside. The worst time of the day was after six in the evening, especially when we would hear, in the distance, people going to the cinema at the Opera House. I was determined that, when freed, nothing would get me back in this place.

After two weeks we were driven in the same vans for trial by Courts Martial at the Royal Court. We sat in a row at the back whilst waiting for it all to commence. The proceedings were conducted by an array of German officers, the sight of whom filled us with dread, but the charges were read out quietly enough and we had to stand while sentences were declared. Barbier and Killer were brought in, also to be tried. Killer hadn't been imprisoned with us but we were told later that it was he who had caused all the trouble by spitting in a Jersey girl's face when she was out with a German officer on the night in question. All of us who were under sixteen years of age were given six months jail but were put on probation because of our ages. Barbier received a longer sentence and was transported to France for two years. He was a very brave and defiant person. I have never understood why his courage had not received some sort of recognition after the war.

My dad and other parents were outside the Royal Court that afternoon when we were released. Back at the Exeter he had prepared a large pie with, I think eggs and bacon and onions. He always loved to cook and reckoned that we would be very hungry by that time. We returned to the pub and tucked in, rather unwisely. Overnight all four of us were violently ill. We were just unused to rich food and had learned a salutary lesson.

Thus 1942 came to an end and what seemed to be the longest year of the Occupation commenced. Although the war news was improving as the Germans were beginning to lose territory, we felt isolated and deserted and that the occupying forces would never leave. The Evening Post was always full of Nazi propaganda and the German UFA news at the cinema was full of their victories, but we were kept up to date with accurate information by the many illicit radios and crystal sets in the hands of Islanders.

We would often go to the West's Cinema to see constant repeats of American films and cartoons and local stage shows, some of which were very good. While there, on occasions we could hear music coming from the Plaza Ballroom next door where the German Forces had a nightclub known as La Belle Ami, which had a rather dubious reputation. Civilians were not permitted to attend the shows which were just open for the German forces and we could imagine the sort of shows that were provided for their men!

We would sometimes get into trouble during the UFA news by jeering at the American sounding lady commentator, especially when she would announce how their troops were just five kilometres from Stalingrad. This came to an end eventually as they never did capture the city. We were also in trouble for making it a rule to sit down during the playing of the German national anthem.

The Occupation Moves On

At this time one had to be very careful to whom, and of what, onespoke. Some Islanders, for one reason or another, would inform on neighbours to the authorities with, on occasions, dire consequences and it was said that members of the German police would chat to youngsters in a friendly manner, offer them sweets, enquiring if Daddy had heard the news lately! It was revealed later that the German police received hundreds of letters from local informers giving details of people who were breaking the laws laid out by the German authorities. Hard to credit that Jersey people could do such reprehensible deeds, but it was said at a later trial that Dr Weissmann, the interpreter, disliked these letters as much as Jersey people did but found the information useful.

By the third year, owing to poor nutrition, lack of vitamins, possibly lack of soap and cleaning materials, cuts, bruises and sores took far longer than normal to heal. At this time my hands became covered with warts and even with potions and ointments from Boots the Chemist across the road from the Exeter, they refused to go away and were quite painful and unsightly for other people. One day our neighbours from the shop across the road, the milliners, Mrs Renouf and Mr and Mrs Poole, with their shop called "Le Petit Louvre", advised me to see a lady called Ruby. She was the sister of their cleaning lady who lived in La Chasse and was renowned for curing warts and other unpleasant ailments by "charming" them. I was, and am still now, a complete sceptic with regard to such matters and it was only after much persuasion that I agreed to pay her a visit with the promise that I would be polite and not laugh at whatever she was about to do. When I arrived at her little terraced house opposite the Forum Cinema, early one evening I was invited in to her parlour and, sitting down, I showed her my hands. She then said that she would cure them for me and proceeded to make signs over the offending sores with quiet incantations. When she had finished and I was about to leave I asked her how long it would be before they would go, expecting her to say, "About six months or more," knowing very well that with luck, they might go on their own accord in this time. "By next week most of them should have disappeared," was her quiet comment. I left, knowing very well that this was most unlikely, but by the time that I visited her on the following Tuesday they had definitely changed and improved and when she took hold of my hands she smoothed the remaining excrescences, leaving the skin beneath clean and healthy! I was astonished and grateful. She then asked me if I had any other ailments. I replied that I had asthma but that I was sure that she couldn't do anything about that, but she made me sit down and repeated the ritual of the previous week. My asthma was never as bad again but I didn't return for further treatment, not believing that such a cure was possible. Later, I wondered that maybe I should have returned and listened to her. Our neighbour, Mrs Poole from "Le Petit Louvre", told me that I mustn't offer her money as she would be offended, "Just take her a nice bunch of flowers," which I did. The healer then told me that the healing was a gift given her by an old lady that she had befriended many years before.

1943 was a comparatively peaceful year for the family. Always feeling hungry was a constant worry, especially for my parents who were concerned about my loss of weight, as I was growing taller but not filling out!

During that year there was a boxing tournament at St Mary and St Peter's church hall between Victoria College and The Beeches. As our school was one short in my weight, I was asked to fill in as I had belonged to a boxing club in Sand Street before the war. I can't remember much about the evening, only that I was thoroughly beaten by one of my College pals by the name of Martin Le Cornu, finishing up home bound for a few weeks with a strained heart, so my doctor said. I don't think that Doctor Mattas, the medical doctor officiating, was over careful of our weakened condition which was due to the lack of nourishing food.

My latest hobby of ornithology seemed to be keeping me out of trouble with the German police. Most spare time was spent in the countryside with Rod Dobson's bird-watching group. We soon discovered areas of cliff tops which were not mined and where the rarer birds like peregrine falcons and ravens flourished. In pre-war days, pigeon fanciers were known to find and shoot peregrine falcons on the north coast in order to protect their racing pigeons. Now, they were not permitted to have shotguns and were unable to get at the nests owing to the minefields.

There was a slight downside to these excursions to the north coast. From promontories like the Col de la Rocque, Sorel or similar vantage points, one could clearly see on the horizon to the north-west the sister islands of Sark, Herm and Guernsey while to the east was the low lying coast of Normandy, the white sands stretching northwards to Cap de la Hague. On fine clear days, to the north a faint smudge on the horizon proved to be the most northerly of our Islands, Alderney. The close proximity of these inaccessible places accentuated our feelings of living in a nine by five mile prison for over three years and we longed to get off of the Island and visit these other places but, at that time, with little hope of getting off and no immediate prospects of liberation.

We did have, however, one or two scares. In March 1943, Pat, Ron Smith (Smut) and I decided to have a look at the raven's nest at Wolf's Caves. These large crows performed wonderful gyrations early in the nesting season and their deep croaks were evocative of the wilderness of the north coast cliffs. Leaving our cycles near an old granite and pantiled hut at the top, we scrambled down the cliff path for a closer look. What we didn't know was that a squad of Jerries was on manoeuvres in the countryside around. Our first intimation of this was when, on returning to our bikes, a stick grenade came sailing through the air and exploded with a loud bang near the hut. Several more followed with machine gun and rifle fire so we quickly rushed away down the cliff path and didn't return until we were sure that they had moved on.

On another occasion Rod Dobson was low-water fishing in the Icho Tower area and hunting for lobster and conger eels, a useful pastime with food in such short supply. Even though he was an Englishman, it was a hobby at which he was an expert. He hadn't noticed the warning about "Scharfschiessen," that is, artillery practice, in the previous night's Evening Post. He had removed his shorts and shirt because of the heat and wandered off in his birthday suit looking into familiar crevices for these fish. Suddenly, a whirring noise and ear-splitting explosions as rocks and sand erupted around Icho tower. He raced away in a great panic dodging from rock to rock, completely starkers, losing all his fishing gear and clothing as he ran towards the shore, or so he told us later, and raced in the direction of Rocqueberg Point. Fortunately, a close friend, Arthur Harrison of the Evening Post was working in his garden. Roderick called out, explaining his predicament and embarrassment and asking for some clothes to wear! Arthur, highly amused, soon came to the rescue; his modesty was preserved and all was well.

The Germans never queried our use of binoculars even when near to their fortifications. To us this seemed to be extremely tolerant but I suppose that they noticed our ages and could see no harm in what we were doing. Roderick had a pair of seven by fifty Carl Zeiss binoculars and I had a pair of German Army six times Zeiss Dienstglass which my brother-in-law had quietly removed whilst on one of his forays on the docks.

Frank told us many stories of acts of sabotage that occurred at the harbours by the dockers, either for patriotism or just gain. On one occasion the Germans had requisitioned radios belonging to Islanders, and these were being taken to France, with the Jersey harbour workers loading them into the hold. Whenever possible each radio was purposely dropped, thereby smashing the fragile valves and making each set valueless to the Germans. The authorities later heard of this sabotage and some locals were charged with malicious damage.

On another occasion Frank told us that sweetbreads from slaughtered cattle were being accumulated in fridges at the abattoir for a special delivery to the High Command in Normandy. The secret of the unusual refrigerated container on the ship was quickly discovered by the men working in the hold and the hungry men soon discovered how to get at this delicacy before its departure for Granville. I had never tasted them before. Floured and fried in butter they were quite delicious, especially as our diet was restricted and food was becoming in such short supply. Later, we were told that there was one almighty row when the refrigerated container was opened and the spoils missing. There were no repercussions in Jersey as it wasn't known whether the goods were stolen in Jersey or on arrival in France. Frank told me one day that a German sentry on duty at the harbours told him that the Channel Islands might be the most peaceful place in Europe but that it was certainly inhabited by the biggest thieves!

On our many bird watching excursions I gradually learned my way painfully around the Island. Painfully, because by now we had hose- pipes for tyres, which made for a very uncomfortable ride! We would often visit the big rookery at Le Gallais' Woods at La Moye Manor, where Rod would climb to the top of the pine trees with climbing irons to count the nests and eggs. With Madame Riley's permission we explored the valleys at Rozel Manor, more trips to Queen's Valley when, on one occasion we noticed again that more large artillery shells had been wired to trees at the top of the cotils ready to be released on invading troops or tanks should they venture up the valley. We kept well away from these dangerous objects. We also learned the names of all the approachable creuxs and gullies on the north coast and saw our first puffins that were nesting on the cliffs at Plemont and at the Grand Becquet. Frequently Roderick would lend one of his pairs of binoculars to all to have a closer view of these beautiful sea birds. On one occasion one of the College girls was unfortunate enough to drop the glasses down the bank and over the cliff. Stranger still, not a word of criticism. Roderick was a very patient and tolerant person.

On November 18th 1942 an R.A.F. Spitfire made a crash landing in a slightly sloping field just north of Victoria Village. The French pilot was uninjured and taken prisoner. We rushed out after school hoping maybe for a souvenir or two but by this time the Germans had placed a guard on the plane which was still tilted on its nose. We were told later that a large crowd had got there first and grabbed a few mementos. We heard a long time after the war that this pilot, a Frenchman, tried to escape from a prisoner of war camp in Germany but was captured and shot by the Gestapo.

It was early in 1943 that one of the parents of three boys at our school, Mr Maurice Le Voguer, pre-war assistant Scout commissioner, came up with the idea of starting a school Scout troop to give another interest to the pupils and possibly keep them out of more trouble with the occupying forces. It was a risky proposition as all youth organizations in the Island were strictly banned, but Brother Edward gave the idea his support, hoping that the scouting activities would keep his fifth form pupils out of the German clutches in the local prison in Gloucester Street where, by now, quite a few were residing. I was given the position of Scoutmaster, having been a boy-scout in 1939 and although we operated without uniforms, the project was a success, with various activities taking place, including a concert at Glenham Hall during January 1945, which was a success and repeated at the Hospital and Dispensary by special request.

Troop meetings came to an end in February well before this time as quite a few of the senior members came under the scrutiny of the Military Police and were residing in H.M.Prison in Gloucester Street.

Christmas 1943 was a sorry time for most Islanders. The official meat ration was small and rabbits and chickens were in great demand as well as black market pork. Many funny stories were bandied about concerning the subterfuges used by farmers and undertakers to move illicit pork from one destination to another in an attempt to avoid the German patrols. It was said that on one or two occasions the undertaker's hearse was used to transport whole pigs to their ultimate destination, definitely not the grave, the carcass occupying the wooden box! Still, some alcohol was obtainable from a small official allocation but mainly illicit supplies came from crews arriving from Granville and St Malo. There were also some bottles of alcohol stolen from German stores and a very potent calvados, never matured sufficiently, and made from surplus cider from some farms. There were many illicit stills hidden on the Island and it was said that Irish poteen, a highly powerful spirit, had been distilled from potato juice! On one occasion a supply of red wine came into the Island for allocation but was so acid that the only thing to do it was to distil it into some sort of spirit.

Toys were mainly home-made or exchanged in the exchange and mart column of the Evening Post. Flour made from potatoes, sugar beet syrup, locally made jelly from carrageen moss, a type of seaweed found at low water on the south coast, tough limpets, and ersatz coffee were all in demand. Most people were constantly hungry and had recourse to the food kitchens set up by a Miss Fraser in St Helier for hungry Islanders. Throughout 1943 food and fuel was in very short supply with more and more restrictions placed on the population. Fuel was difficult to obtain and the Germans had to prohibit the cutting down of trees as parts of the Island were becoming quite denuded. At "Suncote", the green elm logs had to be continually blown with a large pair of bellows to stay alight and, even so, this timber gave little heat.

Time seemed to pass very slowly. We would go to the cinema to see the few American films passed as suitable by the German censor as well as many German films with English sub-titles. I remember two in particular. One was an anti-semitic film called Jew Suss which was particularly unpleasant, the other a marvellous comedy called "Quax der Bruch pilot", with Germany's equivalent to George Formby, the very funny, Heinz Ruhmann. The music to this film was also memorable and one piece "Heimat deine Sterne" is famous to this day. It was said that Dr Goebbels, Reich propaganda minister, encouraged the production of this light-hearted tale to cheer up the German people who were suffering from the dreadful effects of massive Allied air raids.

There was always a background of fear as time went by. People informed on neighbours, either for envy, jealousy or even just revenge. Houses would be searched and radios or illicit food stocks found. On one occasion a large stock of black market food was found at a pharmacy at Snow Hill. The German authorities thought they would show these people up as racketeers by displaying these rather wonderful items in their shop window. We didn't look down on the perpetrators at all; we were just possibly a bit envious! People were imprisoned in the town prison in Gloucester Street, or sent to France and Germany for more serious offences, some never to return.

In November 1943, friends of mine, the Painter family, Clarence and his son Peter were informed on and the German police found a pistol, radio and cameras whilst searching the property. They were sentenced to imprisonment on the Continent where Peter died in late 1944 and his father in February 1945. One of the locals had informed on them. So sad, they were such a fine family.

On the whole most people avoided fraternising with the occupying forces. Naturally there were exceptions. Orviss the fisheries and vegetable store in Halkett Street had to supply certain sections of the occupying forces with vegetables and fish on a daily basis. It was managed by a man called Jackson with Ted Savage as the fishmonger. German officers would come in with their orders during the late morning and some sort of social gathering developed with drinking and socialising in the back office. Poor old Ted Savage hated their visits and my dad refused to visit the shop whenever the German officers were in attendance. Unfortunately, one of the local businessmen in the street who was over fond of his little nip of scotch, would pop in daily and soon the locals heard of these goings on. When the Occupation finally came to an end he was barred from attending the United Services Club for quite a time, which hurt as he was a prominent member, and had served in the British Army as a machine gunner during the Great War. People had long memories.

In May 1943 the German authorities insisted that the German language be taught in the Island schools. Brother Marcel and lay teacher Pat O'Shea were given the task of carrying this out. As neither of them had any knowledge of the language I couldn't go wrong and won the school prize, the only time I had ever been first at any subject. In due course a German officer arrived to make the presentation and after a short propaganda speech in front of the school I was given the first prize. This turned out to be a book, an anti-American volume of slavery in the United States, no illustrations and in German script! As soon as he had left I gave the book to my mate Albert Le Verdier who seemed keen to have it. I regretted this later as it had an inscription inside to the effect that, at last, I had won something!

In May 1944, one of our class by the name of James Houillebecq who lived at Five Oaks had been informed on and his house searched by the Feldgendarmerie once again. They found stolen ammunition and he was imprisoned and tried. Later, he was sent to France and we heard later that he had died in Neuengamme concentration camp in January 1945. All very sad as the war news was much better and it seemed we would finally achieve victory in the end.

By early 1943 the war news seemed to be improving. The first major disaster for the Germans occurred in January with the surrender of their army at Stalingrad. Nearer to home we heard that the Geheime Feld Polizei (Secret Field Police) had moved to 'Silvertide' at Havre des Pas and that address assumed a sinister reputation. More of interest to me was that leading members of the Societe Jersiaise decided to form junior sections and I joined the bird watching group.

On September 8th, Italy surrendered and we had hopes of a quick end to the Occupation but this was not to be. The days, weeks, and months dragged on and, on occasions, in despair we felt that the Germans would be with us forever and that the Occupation would never come to an end.

On November 16th 1943, a British cruiser, H.M.S. Charybdis and destroyer, H.M.S. Limbourne were sunk during a night action between Guernsey and north Brittany coast and many dead sailors were washed up around the Islands and along the French coast. Many locals attended the funerals of these unfortunate men, who were buried in the new military cemetery at Howard Davis Park near St Luke's Church.

We continued to live in hopes that soon there would be an invasion of the French coast but had no idea when this could possibly happen. There were constant rumours of radio messages from a certain Colonel Britain preparing the members of the French Resistance for further acts of sabotage against the German occupiers. Our light naval ships were frequently near the Islands and successfully attacking ships bringing supplies to the Islands.

On June 5th 1944, Ron Smith, Pat McGarry and I decided to visit the north coast in search of seagulls' eggs. It was too late in the season but we still scrabbled around for the fun of it. In one area I became stuck on a very steep damp grassy bank with a sheer cliff below. With help from the other two I was extricated, but with soaking wet trousers from the long grass. We rushed back to town as I had been promised a visit to West's Cinema with my sister Helene and Frank if I was on time. I hadn't the opportunity to change and went in my damp clothing.

There was huge panic overnight with the German troops fully armed and tearing around as something important was occurring. The Allied invasion of Normandy had commenced early that morning. The German soldiers were in full battle uniform, steel helmets, rifles and hand grenades slung around their necks. Although I wasn't feeling too well I rose early and at eight rushed down to the Weighbridge to find out what could be causing all this panic with the troops. Suddenly I began to feel very ill and collapsed against a low wall. Someone noticed my predicament and helped me back to the Exeter where I was sent to bed and the doctor called. Very shortly Doctor Gow arrived and told my parents that I had a very bad bout of pneumonia. Fortunately for me he had just had an issue of some new tablets known as M and B. Later we were told that they were the new drug called penicillin and that they had just arrived in time to bring my temperature down. Although I felt rotten, I didn't realise how seriously ill I was, that is, until the parish priest arrived at the request of my mother to give me the last sacraments. That really gave me a scare! I insisted that I didn't feel that bad and didn't want all this fuss made as I wanted to be out in a short time and watching the defeat of the German Army. What I regretted most of all was missing the excitement of the Normandy battles which I could have seen from the east coast, having waited so long for this all to happen, but I was several vital weeks out of action and missed all the excitement.

I was told later that, on June 9th, four German soldiers, on guard at La Rocque and returning from duty at Seymour Tower, had wandered out on the wet sand at low water, hadn't noticed the rapidly rising tide and had become surrounded by the incoming sea. Mike Le Clercq and Bob Kempster, local fishermen wanted to launch a boat to rescue them but were forbidden to do so. This occurred just after the Normandy invasion and the military was jittery and afraid to take help from the locals. The Germans later launched their own boat from Gorey but were too late and the four soldiers drowned, to be found later on the outgoing tide belted together as a last resort for safety. It was such a sad story.

One day, in September 1944, McClusky was chatting to my dad in the bar as he used to do after work. These were times of great mistrust amongst the population. Some people, for one reason or another, would settle old scores by sending anonymous letters to the German authorities to obtain revenge for past aggravations or out of envy for various reasons. It was said in the Von Aufsess Occupation Diary that the German authorities received hundreds of anonymous letters informing the police of infractions of their regulations but that many of them were ignored and destroyed. In talking, McClusky mentioned something disturbing which got my dad thinking and he decided to take actions which were to have strange and worrying repercussions. He was talking about our mainland friends from the Church. He advised Dad to be careful about what we said to them in the future. The reasons he gave were that he had, on occasions, to deliver supplies to Geheime Feld Polizei headquarters at "Silvertide", Havre des Pas, as part of his job. He implied that he had seen the gentleman in question frequently in this establishment, that he seemed to be too friendly with the occupants, and was just warning Dad to be careful what he spoke about in the future. Life was like that at the time. It was unwise to trust anybody.

Strangely enough, apart from Church on a Sunday, we weren't seeing a great deal of this family by now. They seemed to be much occupied with their own activities and purchasing second hand motor cars or so we were told. I was told later that they had a large heap of rubbish piled high in the forecourt of their hotel as if they had something hidden beneath. Because of what McClusky had told us Dad then decided to ask the gentleman in question to remove his mattresses from the cellar, implying diplomatically that, as the war was likely to be ending in the not too distant future, the brewery would not take too kindly to other people's belongings being stored in our cellar. The gentleman wasn't at all pleased with this request and agreed to move them as soon as possible, replying rather abruptly that he would move them sometime the following week.

True to his word, one afternoon in the following week he turned up with the two boys and a handcart, and as my dad was out my mother let him in and down the cellar. The mattresses were moved out of the front hatch and on to the cart. On leaving he called my mother down to lock up and as he did so he warned her that Dad had some bottles of forbidden spirits with the German insignia on the labels, hidden in the cellar. My mother replied that she had nothing to do with the management of the business but that she would tell him when he arrived back from the country. Dad came back at about five-thirty and was given the warning which unfortunately he carelessly ignored.

At six there was a knock on the front door and I followed him down to see who was there. To my horror there were two young German under-officers asking to examine the cellar. Without choice

Dad disappeared down with them to emerge a few minutes later. Each officer was carrying a bottle wrapped in newspaper and Pop with a very relieved look on his face. Tongue in cheek they had pointed out the forbidden spirits but said that, as the Island was now completely cut off from, France and that the situation was rapidly changing, they would not proceed to charge my dad with the infringements,--- but please could they each buy a bottle! And when Dad happily agreed they insisted on paying! Truth can be stranger than fiction, but - coincidence!!!?

In October 1944, one Sunday morning I returned from Church to be told by my dad that the Feldgendarmerie had called, searched the pub once again, especially my room, ripping the mattress, pulling up loose floorboards and up the chimney as if looking for something in particular. They found nothing of interest and didn't even comment about my Army first aid box which they re-opened and examined. On leaving they told Dad that I was to present myself at "Silvertide", Havre des Pas, Geheime Feld Polizei H.Q. at eight o'clock on the Monday morning. The family was naturally worried, that is until I explained that I had done nothing wrong for many months as I spent all of my spare time bird watching.

The next morning the family insisted on giving me sandwiches in case I finished up in Gloucester Street jail once again. I walked down and arrived promptly at eight, to be invited in and told to sit down to be interrogated.

There were several German police in the room, now in army uniform under their shiny mackintoshes, their usual plain clothes outfits. They stared at me, one cleaning his automatic pistol, possibly to put the fear of God into me, and with great success. The officer interviewing me was handling a piece of writing paper. I believe his name was Woelfle. His first comment was, "Mr Le Cocq, I would like you to return to us your Mauser automatic pistol." This statement came as a complete shock as I hadn't seen my pistol for many months as it was hidden in my brother-in-law's cellar. My immediate reply was "I haven't got a gun. My father wouldn't permit me to own one and in any case, how would I obtain one? "Mr Le Cocq, we know you have a gun as it is written in this letter by one of your friends." He refused to show me the letter. I continued to deny owning a gun so Woelfle said that I would be taken to prison until they got it back.

With that they marched me out and bundled me into the back of their Citroen Light fifteen car and was driven to jail. As we drove down Queen Street and past the Exeter, Mum and Dad were on the doorstep, she looking very worried, possibly a tear or two, but I did get a feeble wave.

I was taken to a small darkened cell in the German section, to solitary confinement. I was then checked over by a German medical orderly and was rather amazed as, instead of the usual stethoscope as used by Jersey doctors, he tested my chest with a primitive wooden one. A tubby German warder, by the name of Otto, was the man in charge. He seemed quite congenial and asked me if I would like to see one of my school mates who was in the next cell to mine. I was taken to the adjacent cell to find one of my school pals, Dickie Williams, lying on his mattress, both ankles bandaged and in quite a lot of pain. He gave me his usual grin, told me that he was starving, so I gave him my sandwiches as his need was certainly far greater than mine.

It turned out that, a few days before, he, Donald Bell, and Frank Le Pennec had organised an escape. According to what Dickie said,

114

they had tied up their blankets in a form of rope and in the middle of the night had rung the cell bell for Otto as if needing to go to the toilet. As Otto arrived, half asleep, they bundled him in to the cell, tied him up, rushed out, and locked the cell door with Otto inside. On each other's backs they climbed the prison wall, Dickie being the last. By this time Otto had pressed the alarm bell, had been released and was in the courtyard and firing his pistol at the last of the escapees. Donald and Frank rushed away but Dick fell heavily on the outside pavement injuring his ankles, and had to crawl away, hoping to evade capture. I think he reached Westmount before being caught by the German police, roughed up for causing the trouble and taken to the hospital for attention. He was now my neighbour for a week and as usual, good company, saying how kind the nurses had been to him when he had been admitted by the German police.

Two days after my incarceration, our so-called friends from the mainland visited the Exeter with the two boys to commiserate with my parents and to offer to check my room once again to see if any forbidden article had been missed by the German police. In his naivety, my father, even though we hadn't been in touch with them for some time, accepted their offer and my bedroom was searched once again. On seeing my British Army first-aid box, the boys' father said that they had better look after it for me "in case it would get me into further trouble" and promptly took it away, my father, without thinking, accepting the offer.

I was now in solitary confinement, in a small dark cell with a high window which was impossible to reach. During this depressing time there was someone in the cell above who paced around for the whole of the time I was there, that is, until one day the pacing suddenly stopped. I was told later that it was a German soldier who had molested a Jersey girl and was later taken out and executed. How true this was I will never know. I never saw him.

A week later, I was collected once again in the Citroen and driven back to "Silvertide". Quietly, but menacingly once again, Woelfle asked me about the pistol. He told me again that he had a letter from an informer to prove it but still wouldn't show it to me. When I continually denied any knowledge of the weapon he said that I would go back to the cell while they searched all the homes of my relatives. This came as a shock and I became very worried as I knew that my brother-in-law, Frank, had my pistol as well as a Lee-Enfield rifle, a radio and a live pig in the basement of the house they were renting called "Le Cotil", on Wellington Road. Frank was used to farm animals, having worked on a sheep station in South Australia in the thirties and was hoping to supplement the rations with some illegal pork. I knew about the pig and it had been rather amusing at times, watching German soldiers pushing their bikes up Wellington Road, pausing to sniff the farmyard smell and possibly hearing the odd grunt coming from the ventilator. Sometime later, when the animal was big enough, I had to watch from the raised garden to make sure that no-one was on the hill whilst Frank slaughtered it, a rather noisy and messy procedure and then shaved all the hairs off with a sharp knife and hot water! I didn't like that bit.

I then had to admit that I had possessed the gun a long time past but had put it in a box and buried it in a field for safety. The German now satisfied that he was getting somewhere with me then told me to tell them where it was so that they could dig it up. I refused saying that if they would send my father down to see me in Gloucester Street I would tell him where to find it. He agreed to this suggestion and later I told my dad where to find the missing pistol. He collected the gun from Frank, delivered it to "Silvertide" and, true to their word, on receiving the weapon I was released until the time of my trial. I was told at a later date, that by this time, the war was going against them and that they didn't want a crowd of hot-headed armed youths taking revenge with firearms when the Occupation finally came to an end.

A week later we had another phone call from "Silvertide" telling me to pay them visit on the following morning. They told my parents that I wasn't in any more trouble but that they wanted to ask me some questions. Next morning I arrived promptly as usual and was invited politely inside and told to take a seat. Wölfle once again, "Mr Le Cocq, you have a school friend by the name of Baton? He also has a gun, is now in jail and whenever we tell him that he will be released if it is returned, he just laughs at us. I would like you to go to the prison and tell him that he will be released if he returns his gun."

Once again I was bundled into the Citroen light-fifteen (known after the war as a Maigret car, after the famous detective) and taken through town to the prison and to Baton's cell. This was in the civilian section far from where I had been imprisoned, and where he was sharing a cell with two Frenchmen who couldn't speak a word of English whilst Dougie didn't know a word of French. I was told later that the conversation and language between the three was something wonderful to be heard and a great entertainment to the other prisoners. I did as I was told and told him that he would be released when they got the gun back. He was quite alarmed. My dad gave me a hiding when he found that I had the gun and threw it out into the sea, saying, "You will have to tell him to find another one." I then left and walked to the market to give Mr Baton the news. He had a locksmith's shop facing Beresford Street in the Central Market and was working there when I arrived. He was, of course, furious but said that he would try to get hold of a gun to keep the Jerries happy. He did so and a few days later delivered an old antique pistol, with ammunition that didn't fit, to "Silvertide" but it satisfied Wölfle and Doug was released. There were quite a few funny stories from the youthful occupants of His Majesty's Prison in Gloucester Street which were bandied around for some time later. Otto the tubby little head warder, a private in the German Army, had an endearing call in the morning to rouse his schoolboy occupants. At an early time he would rattle a metal plate or tin shouting at the same time in his halting English, "Raus, raus pisspot mit," to the great amusement of all concerned!

A few weeks later Doug and I were summoned to the German Court at Westbourne Terrace on Wellington Road where we were put on trial by a small group of officers. After a brief summary of the charge we were each sentenced to six months in Gloucester Street jail for being in possession of forbidden firearms. We realised how lucky we were. Six months earlier, before D-Day, for such an offence we would have been sent to France for imprisonment or even shot, but now that the war was going so badly for the German Forces the sentences didn't seem to be so serious. They then told us that, when there were vacancies at the prison, we would be told to report to Gloucester Street with blankets and a pillow! The local jail at that time was filled to overflowing with many locals who had got into trouble. The war came to an end a few months later and Doug and I still have six months to do!

A few weeks after my release I asked my dad if I could have my first aid box back from our so-called friends from the Church. He approached the gentleman after Mass on the following Sunday to be told that this wasn't possible as they had found the box full of German ammunition and that they had thrown it away. I was livid. This was absolutely untrue but we could do nothing about it. I just didn't trust them and haven't spoken to them to this day.

From the time that the Allies had advanced down the Normandy peninsular the food situation had become precarious as the ports of Granville and St Malo were now inaccessible for German supply ships. We were now using sea water for cooking the few vegetables available and those were mainly swedes. For heating we had sawdust mixed with pitch which ruined most town fireplaces. Supplies of gas and electricity were restricted. Islanders were cold and hungry and many were suffering from malnutrition. It was said that it was only the supply of fresh Jersey milk that prevented the situation from being dire. The soldiers were just as hungry as we were. Cats and dogs disappeared from the streets and it certainly wasn't the civilian population who were eating them. My pals and I joined the St John's Ambulance Brigade for want of something better to do and attended lectures at the Hospital from a Doctor Darling and instruction at the Brigade headquarters.

The situation was saved at Christmas 1944 by the arrival of the Red Cross ship, Vega, with supplies of food parcels. As I was now a member of St John's Ambulance Brigade I participated in the collection of these goods by having to accompany the German soldier drivers of the horse-driven drays when the boxes were collected from the quays. The population were ecstatic as they contained such articles as powdered egg and milk, white soap, sugar and milk chocolate, as well as other items that we hadn't seen for years.

The first arrival was December 30th, just a bit late for Christmas, but it didn't matter. We were saved from starvation and there were further deliveries until June 1945. I think the amazing thing about the arrival of these parcels was that the Germans never interfered with the delivery of all this wonderful food even though they themselves were starving. So much for their discipline.

All the same we felt frustrated as so many parts of Europe were being liberated, and it seemed, once again, as if we had been forgotten. By this time I was helping with teaching at my school as there was such a shortage of proper staff. The first occasion for this new activity was when Brother Edward, the head, said in desperation, "Kevin, leave your studies and take 2b for the morning." Arriving at the end class room I found myself in charge of eighty-five, eleven to thirteen year old tearaways, most eager to get the better of me. However, I managed to keep control, endeavoured to get them studying with dire threats but was nearly a nervous wreck by the end of the week! Whether they learned anything or not was a debatable point! Terry might have the answer! Some of this original class still contact me when they visit south-west Australia.

Coming home from school one day in January 1945, I decided to call on my sister at her home at Le Cotil in Wellington Road. By this time she had a young girl helper as she had the three boys to cope with as well as her little shop on Burrard Street. As I entered the kitchen I was shocked to find a German soldier sitting there having a cup of tea or coffee and chatting away to this girl. He was typically German, fair haired, blue eyed, very friendly and seemed keen to talk. He was dressed in what looked like, for me, an unusual black uniform, no jackboots and had a black sponge-padded beret. He explained that he was a tank driver and was the boyfriend of the girl helper. I was nonplussed. This was the first time that our family had had anything to do with the occupying forces, a friendly German on the property, apart from the many interrogations, I felt a bit of a traitor and left as soon as it was possible. I think that it was a principle of most Jersey people to have as little as possible to do with the enemy forces throughout the Occupation. This was passive resistance but on occasions some of my younger pals and I thought that it was a bit chicken livered of our authorities for not putting up a much stronger resistance to the Germans in some form or other. Unfortunately, most of them seemed to settle back and not provoke them in any form or other, choosing anything for peace and quiet rather than possible reprisals from the German authorities.

At the beginning of August 1944, during mid morning, hundreds of bombers flew South over the Island and we watched them from our school yard. They were flying very high and producing vapour trails, a phenomenon we hadn't observed before. The German flak gunners didn't open fire until the last planes were overhead and they were soon out of sight. We heard later that they were about to bomb concentrations of German troops in what was known as the Falaise gap, an area in Normandy where large numbers of their troops were surrounded.

It was early in 1944 that I first met Reg. I think that he was our milkman at the time, delivering milk to the Exeter with his milk cart. He was a cheerful but, at times, a worrying individual but always happy and whistling most of the time because he had a passion for classical music. We would meet on occasions at the bathing pool and it was he who introduced me to a family of equally enthusiastic lovers of classical music. The older brother was Harry, who, I believe was a painter and decorator, then Len who worked at the Evening Post. They had other friends of like interest who I would meet when invited to their home to listen to some of their wonderful collection of gramophone records. As time went on I learned, without realising it, that Reg had introduced me to the nucleus of the Communist Party in the Island although he wasn't a Communist himself and was inclined to poke fun at their ardent beliefs. Reg and I always treated it as a joke when they would greet each other with clenched right fists and the greeting, "Workers of the world unite and the rich shall grind in the face of the poor!" We had to listen, ad nauseum on occasions, to expressions of admiration for Joseph Stalin and Russia, the wonder country whose soldiers were winning the war for the allies. However, it was obvious that their enthusiasm for the war was only stirred after the invasion of Russia by the Germans and I think that before that time, if the occasion had necessitated it, they would have been conscientious objectors. However, they were sincere and kindly people, even if misguided, and I enjoyed their company and their music.

One day, Len asked me to teach him to swim and I agreed to do my best and down to the pool we went. We commenced his lessons in the summer of 1944 and he was grateful for my efforts, especially when, on one occasion he dog-paddled out of his depth, began to panic and flounder until I swam out, grabbed his arm and pulled him to safety. Strangely enough he seemed to be eternally in my debt for saving him from a watery demise and always reminded me of this fact, which was, of course, quite unnecessary. Later, I jokingly told him that this was one of the greatest mistakes of my life!

I am mentioning this small part of my Occupation activities as I found, after a time, that their beliefs and attitudes to most subjects were quite astounding and rather worrying. This passive non-argumentative attitude on my part came to a head when there were quite a number of their associates present when I was in their company.

On this occasion, after the war in 1947, the subject of the Berlin airlift was mentioned and I remarked casually that I thought that the Russians were being unreasonable, considering that they had been our allies throughout the war. Len turned on me in fury saying that if there was to be war between Russia and the Western Allies, he would go to Russia and join the Russian Army in order to fight with them against the capitalistic British and Americans. I don't think, and hoped, that he didn't mean it and the subject was soon forgotten. It just gave one food for thought on how fanatical they were, how their minds worked and how dangerous this attitude could be. Nevertheless, we remained good friends until his death, a few years ago, even after I had ridiculed his comments.

It was about this time that we noticed a strange occurrence with the troops that seemed amusing at the time. From the 26th, or 27th of July in 1944 there seemed to be a certain atmosphere amongst them at the pool. From an easy going attitude that had been prevailing, they suddenly changed from giving the normal military salute to the stiff "Heil Hitler" arm raised affair. We soon found out that an attempt to assassinate the Fuehrer had been made by certain Army officers and all members of the armed forces had now to show their loyalty in this manner. I think that some soldiers took the order seriously, whereas others made a bit of a joke of having to do so. The salute very soon returned to normal. I stupidly put my foot in it at the time when arriving at the pool one afternoon without noticing that there were quite a few sunbathing soldiers amongst our crowd. As I approached my pals I clicked my heels, put my right arm up and said "Heil Churchill" Our crowd froze. I then realised my mistake as I received several frigid stares from some of their crowd. I sat down quietly, hoping that there were no ardent Nazis amongst them. Nothing more was said, but I was a lot more careful in the future.

One of our bathing-pool crowd was a slightly older individual by the name of Curley Dimond. Well built, a strong swimmer and on the whole popular with everyone, he had that one quality which made him of great interest in certain circumstances. We were given to understand that his mother was from Alsace Lorraine in Eastern France, on the border with Germany. He was raised there, spoke fluent German as well as French and of course, now that he was living in Jersey spoke English like one of us. Not once, to our knowledge did he ever let on that, whilst at the pool he could understand what the German soldiers were talking about to each other which proved of great interest to us later when he would give us the gist of their conversations. It was he who had told us the reason for their temporary change of salute. During the time since their arrival and their constant use of Havre des Pas bathing pool, the German occupiers had never interfered with our activities at the pool or tried to force their friendship on to us or our crowd of girls. We never included them in our competitions and water polo matches and had as little to do with them as possible. On the whole, they were quietly well behaved and mannered. There were no boorish activities that sometimes occupy men or women when in a crowd. It was just that they were here; we were not free and were subject to every condition that they had placed on the population. We just wanted them out so that we could return to normal living, free from the threats from the military police, of constant hunger and fear of imprisonment for mundane infringements like possession of a radio and, worst of all, being sent to a prison in France, often with dire consequences.

It was in October 1944 that Jimmy Thelland, Ronnie Baucher and I were invited with Ron's sisters to a College girl's party at a large dairy farm in St Saviour. It had to be an all-night party owing to the curfew, and Jimmy, having just had his appendix removed, had to go

124

on Ron's cross-bar as he was not allowed to cycle and didn't wish to miss the occasion. It was a good party, no alcohol, and drugs hadn't been heard of. We had lots of fun and heaps of wonderful food! Our eyes bulged at the sight of items we hadn't seen for years. However, you don't look a gift horse in the mouth so we got on and enjoyed ourselves. As the evening activities came to an end we became tired and a bit sleepy. Some relaxed in armchairs, others played cards to while away the time until the dawn.

As we were about to leave, the mother of the girl whose birthday it was came in and said that we couldn't leave before breakfast and were led into the large kitchen dining room where a wonderful spread was laid out for us to tuck into. We just couldn't believe it, eggs, bacon, jam, scones, white bread a huge block of butter and tea or real coffee! They were so kind and we now realised why the farmer himself had a rather rotund figure and that he hadn't been too short of food for the past four years. We were most appreciative but I suppose, a little later, rather critical.

It was about this time that several small groups of the younger members of the population were planning escapes from the Island in order to take part in the war. The coast of Normandy was only about sixteen miles away at the nearest point and escape was now not as hazardous as the French coast was in Allied hands. I had thought of joining one of these groups when I came out of jail, but was afraid that my parents would be the ones to suffer when my absence was discovered so I decided against it. It was a dangerous activity as the soldiers would not hesitate to fire upon escapees if their attempts were discovered. Most of the College and other Jersey lads were successful, but some were captured and imprisoned and some lost their lives in the dangerous waters that surround the Island.

The constant memories of the latter months of 1944 and the first few months of 1945 seemed to be that of being hungry and cold. On Sundays we would take trays of potatoes and swedes to Mr Egre, the baker in Duhamel Place as both the electricity and gas were switched off at intervals. The timber to keep warm was green and gave little heat. I am told that there are certain Islanders who, even now, cannot face cooked swedes. We also had a supply of pitch to mix with sawdust and burn in the fireplaces, ruining the tiles completely.

It seemed as if the Germans would never surrender. Retreating on all fronts it was as if we were forgotten, but life had to go on. At school I had to continue attempting to keep order with my mob of thirteen and fourteen year old pupils and follow the curriculum as much as possible. On March 7th I left my classroom at mid-day and was walking across the playground when there was a huge explosion from the direction of Bagatelle Road and I felt the blast which followed the frightening noise. There were no windows broken at the school, but the large front windows of Le Gallais shop in Bath Street and other properties in the town were blown out. As there were still smaller explosions taking place, accompanied with the crackle of small arms ammunition, it was decided to send all pupils home for the remainder of the day. We were told later that it was an ammunition dump at the Palace Hotel that had exploded and the hotel partially destroyed. It was rumoured that it had been sabotaged by disaffected members of the German forces but we never did get an authenticated version as to what had occurred.

On the night of March 9th there was further excitement when the Germans sent a commando raiding party of several ships including the two minesweepers that had been in St Helier's Harbour, to raid the French port of Granville. At the time we knew nothing about the oncoming event except that there were various speculations as to why the Germans were shortening the masts of the two minesweepers. We were told later that the attack was a complete surprise to the Americans who were occupying the port. It was more of a morale booster for the German forces. A collier, the Eskwood, was captured and though empty of coal, brought back about thirty American prisoners of war. Fifty-five of their own men were released to return to Jersey to starvation rations! The raid was a complete success but, with casualties on both sides although the ship was only in ballast having just landed its cargo. The Americans were imprisoned in huts on South Hill and Pat McGarry and I were able to accompany Father Dwyer, the parish priest, who visited the camp, to say Mass for the Catholic prisoners each Sunday morning. This was all very satisfying, to be able to talk to these American soldiers, people who hadn't been stuck with us for nearly five years. We were able to chat to the prisoners after the service, hear all the latest news, take them packets of tobacco from some of our locals and also, a week or two later, I took a secret message to be given to an American who was imprisoned in the local jail in Gloucester Street. I can't remember any of the details of how the message reached him, or that someone would collect the message from me at St Mary's and St Peter's Church. The Americans were a light-hearted bunch and aggravated their guards as much as possible.

Most of the excitement for the first few months of 1945 was working with St John's Ambulance Brigade collecting the Red Cross parcels from the 'Vega' and delivering them to the stores along the Esplanade before they were distributed to the starving population. The war was obviously coming to an end. There was much speculation amongst the population. Would the Germans surrender when their armies in Europe were defeated? In February there were rumours that an ardent Nazi Admiral by the name of Hüffmeier had taken over the command of the Islands from General Rudolf Graf Von Schmettow, our Commandant for the past five years, that he would never surrender and that his troops would fight to the death to defend the Islands against the allies. We were apprehensive as to the possible consequences if they decided to fight and many shopkeepers in St Helier decided to have shutters constructed to protect their shopfronts should fighting occur. As we had rather beautiful Victorian frosted glass windows with Exeter Inn inscribed in the glass my dad decided to have shutters made to protect these windows and at great expense employed a local carpenter for their construction. They were to be fastened top and bottom with two large nuts and bolts and were soon ready to be placed in position. When the day arrived for their trial it seemed that the lower bolt on the right window proved to be a bit stubborn in entering the hole in the window frame. My dad, rather impatiently decided to give the bolt a slight clout with a lump hammer to ease its entry. Suddenly there was a splintering crash and when the shutter was finally eased from the wall it was seen that the offending bolt had smashed a splintered hole in the beautiful glass window. For once in a lifetime my father's words were unprintable, the shutters were never replaced and the timber used for fire lighting in the following few weeks! The window stayed in this cracked condition until the front of the building was altered in 1950.

At last, in April 1945, we saw that the European war was just coming to an end. France, Belgium and Holland, Italy and other parts of Europe had been liberated; the Russians were at the gates of Berlin whilst the Allies were advancing across Germany and Austria. Many German towns and cities had been destroyed by allied bombing. Jersey people were discussing the various victories against Germany openly in the streets yet the Germans occupying the Islands seemed to be oblivious to the situation in their country. At least, that was the impression they were hoping us to believe.

We were constantly waiting for news that the Islands would soon surrender to the Allies and that we would be liberated after five tedious years of military occupation. The prison in Gloucester Street was filled to capacity, mainly with local youths, and the Germans took over the Chelsea Hotel, also in Gloucester Street, on April 6th, as an annex to the main prison. Because of this, Doug Baton and I were expecting at any moment to be ordered to this new annex with our blankets and pillows to commence our six months sentence.

On April 7th the German military band gave a public concert in the Royal Square as if all was going well for Germany's war, with Jersey adults and youngsters listening with red, white and blue rosettes in their buttonholes, an activity which would have been put down a few months before by members of the military police. On April 9th I was on duty once again accompanying a German soldier with a horse and dray for the collection of Red Cross parcels from the Albert Pier.

Back at school on the 11th with further noisy explosions as the soldiers completed the demolition of the partially destroyed Palace Hotel. On the 14th another military band concert in the Royal Square to show us, I suppose, that nothing had changed.

On April 20th, Hitler's birthday was celebrated with an even more important concert in the Royal Square and at the Forum Cinema. Regardless of the situation, the German police were still active imposing their laws, even giving fines for cycling offences like riding two abreast! The dreaded Feldgendarmerie were still to be seen on patrol in the streets, their greatcoats, steel helmets and metal plaque on a chain around the necks making it obvious that they were still on top and there to keep the peace and for us not to contravene their laws.

On April 28th there was another open air concert in the Royal Square, but on the 29th great excitement for the civilian population when we heard on the B.B.C. of offers of unconditional surrender being made on the part of the German High Command to Generals Montgomery and Eisenhower in Northern Germany. Would our German garrison ever surrender? In the town there were reports of starving soldiers begging for food from door to door. Yet we now had sufficient to keep going with the help of the Red Cross parcels which were now arriving in the Island at regular intervals. It does say something of the discipline of these soldiers in not stealing some of this food for themselves.

On May 1st there was a big gathering of soldiers at the Forum Cinema. Late that night news came through of Hitler's death. On May 2nd many soldiers filled the town, very quiet and subdued and, we imagined, looking very glum. The swastika flags were flying at half mast and the Forum, their cinema in the Island, closed for a week of mourning.

On May 4th there were the usual rumours of a possible German surrender. People were becoming excited and we were told that the Secret Police at their H.Q. at "Silvertide" had changed from civilian outfits into military uniform and had moved out from their notorious headquarters at Havre des Pas and had integrated into normal military units.

On May 6th many people were circulating around the town and announcements on the B.B.C. told people that the war would end in a day or two. Yet, in the Island there was outwardly no slackening off in war preparations, more gun emplacements and defences still being manned and it was even rumoured that the two minesweepers in the harbour (One had been lost in Granville) were being prepared for further activities! It was so bizarre. Berlin was surrounded by the Russians, the British, French and Americans advancing into Germany with their towns and cities destroyed by Allied bombing! Yet, it seemed that the forces in the Channel Islands were still intending to fight to the end.

On May 8th. everything changed. The Bailiff made a public announcement that the Prime Minister, Winston Churchill, was to make an important announcement at three pm that day. The schools were closed, people poured excitedly into the town buying and waving Union Jacks, and loudspeakers appeared on window sills, in the Royal Square and outside of Bob Lawrence's shop in Charing Cross, as well as in The Parade, in order that everyone could hear the Prime Minister's speech.

I was in The Parade with the horse and dray with my German driver at 3pm when we stopped; as we drew to a halt everyone became quiet in order to hear the momentous words that were to be spoken by Winston Churchill, the Prime Minister.

There is no doubt that few people in the Island, listening to his words were not affected emotionally when he said, "Our dear Channel Islands are to be freed today." People were cheering and shouting with excitement, so much so that one could not hear the remainder of his speech. My driver sat quietly, not really understanding what Churchill's words meant to the people in the Island, but he must have guessed. The five long tedious years of occupation were finally coming to an end.

When I had finished my shift on the parcels I rushed down to the Esplanade hoping to see Allied ships in the bay. No warships, only the arrival, once again, of the Red Cross ship 'Vega' on its fifth visit with more welcome supplies and parcels. The town was still crowded with excited civilians but we had to wait another day for liberation.

The next morning, May 9th 1945, I was out early and down to the Esplanade hoping to see a fleet of Allied ships in the bay. Nothing to be seen at first; however, at ten o'clock a destroyer came around Noirmont point and anchored in the bay. It had happened at last. The Germans were about to surrender.

The Bailiff and authorities had asked for calm. Nevertheless, the town that day and onto the evening was full of excited noisy people. There were no soldiers to be seen, but later some girls with reputations for being collaborators were chased screaming down Queen Street pursued by an unruly crowd of young civilians.

I decided that now was the time to burgle the German store next door, made out of bounds by my father many months before. Maybe the Austrian caretaker had left his sporting rifle behind when he had fled the Island. I was quickly up on to the roof and through the next door skylight into what had been Edna's the bakery before the war. The rooms were still full of domestic and catering equipment but little else. I helped myself to a few articles that might be of use to the family, then spotted a Verey signal pistol with cartridge ammunition which I took for a souvenir and in no time I was back home presenting the booty to my dad.

"Now just you take all of this stuff back and put it back where you found it. It may have been German equipment before but is now the possession and property of the British government!" I was stunned and furious at my father's excessive honesty and we had rather strong words between us, a very unusual occurrence between my dad and me. However, I did as I was told, took everything back except the Verey pistol and ammunition and vented my anger that evening by spending my time on the roof firing red and green cartridges into the evening sky. On firing the pistol the first time I was surprised at the kick back from the pistol when I first pulled the trigger and was more careful with the remainder of the ammunition. The sequel to this episode occurred a few days later when the liberating forces came ashore to terminate the five year occupation of the only part of Great Britain to have been occupied by the Germans and to clear the Island of all signs of the Occupation.

News soon got around that the main liberating force, code named Force135 was to land on Saturday May 12th. Everyone was excited at the prospect of the liberators coming ashore. It was then that my family heard the amazing news, seemingly impossible at first, that my brother Bernard, away from the Island for the previous five years was part of the liberating force and would be coming ashore some time that day.

On Saturday May 12th, I was out early, and decided to walk down Pier Road and watch the forces coming ashore. It was a warm sunny day, there were several ships in the bay and there were R.A.F. planes flying over St.Aubin's Bay and I recognised a Sunderland flying boat and a flight of Spitfires as they flew low giving us a wonderful display. I waited at the top of the steps watching these strange amphibious landing craft called DUKWs coming through the pier heads, full of troops and driving up on to the shingle in front of the old lifeboat shed. Soldiers poured out of these vehicles and lined up in the road and marched up in groups towards the town. Suddenly, in between one of these sections I spotted an officer in naval uniform, also marching towards the town. I immediately recognised the walk, a family peculiarity, and in a trice I was down the steps and greeting my brother after five long years away. It was simply marvellous but I still can't imagine his feelings, stepping ashore, home after five enforced years of absence from his home in Jersey. We had a quick greeting and an excited chat as he had heard several stories about me on the previous night, one that I had been shot, the other that I was still in jail! We then walked directly to the Exeter where my mum and dad were waiting to greet their sailor son after being so long away. It was a wonderful occasion never to be forgotten.

We quickly learned that Bernard, now a Paymaster Lieutenant, was secretary to Captain Fremantle and Commander T.Le B. Pirouet, officers commanding the naval detachment about to land from the troopship, Royal Ulsterman, now anchored in St Aubin's Bay. Being local, Bernard was first of his party to land with orders to obtain billets for the naval and Royal Marine contingent who were about to come ashore.

We heard a story later that he, a very excited Channel Islander, returning home after five years away, was celebrating quite liberally in the ship's wardroom during the voyage across the Channel. Thinking that this momentous occasion warranted it, he sent his orderly to Captain Fremantle and Commander Pirouet insisting that they attend to listen to him playing part of Beethoven's "Moonlight Sonata" on the ship's piano. The ship had left Plymouth on the previous night and as everyone was in a state of semi-euphoria they acquiesced, fully aware of the reasons for his excitement. The ship was now anchored in Aubin's Bay and the liberators were waiting to come ashore.

Bernard quickly told me to get into my Scout's uniform and made Jimmy Thelland and myself ex-officio members of Force 135 and on the Royal Navy pay roll!

We returned immediately to the Weighbridge where there was a big gathering of liberating forces that had just come ashore with excited crowds milling around enjoying the wonder of the occasion. From here we went to the Royal Yacht Hotel, recently vacated by the Kriegsmarine and Bernard decided that the place would be suitable as billets for the naval contingent, even though the kitchens were poorly equipped. As soon as a batch of Germans had been brought in to clean up the place which had been left in quite a filthy condition, they took up residence for the next few weeks.

We returned to the Exeter for a further get together and whilst chatting to my dad, Bernard enquired if we knew of any German stores that might have more catering equipment for their new billet, the Royal Yacht Hotel.Without a second thought my dad told him about the store adjacent to the Exeter and, to my horror, told him to help himself as if he knew all about its contents! Later that day, an Army truck with half a dozen British sailors arrived outside, piled in, opened the first floor French windows and all my booty went out to equip the kitchens at the naval billet! I just couldn't believe it. However, all was not lost as when the Navy left for England at the end of July, I was given much of the equipment for my school Scout troop.

Bernard chose an office on the first floor overlooking the Weighbridge and harbours. As well as employing Jimmy and me as guides and messengers he had a naval writer by the name of Cook as a secretary and Jimmy's sister Jehanne as a typist. There were about eighty members of the naval and marine contingent, from Captain

Fremantle and Jerseyman, Commander T Le B Pirouet, down to Ordinary Seamen and Marines, their task was to clear up mines, ammunition and naval guns that were everywhere. For the next few weeks, the hotel was run like a ship with the traditional Navy disciplines. One tradition which Jim and I found highly amusing was at mid-day when the call went out, "Up spirits" for the daily issue of grog. What never failed to interest us was when some wag would always reply "Stand fast the Holy Ghost!"

It was about this time that Jimmy and I received a salutary lesson in life which rather shook us at the time. Across the road from the Royal Yacht Hotel was another small hotel called the Finsbury. It had been a German naval billet before the Liberation and was now occupied by the British military police, a large Redcap being on duty daily at the main entrance. Very soon quite a few girls would gather around these soldiers and would be invited inside. We knew that two of these girls had not long been discharged from the V.D. clinic at the hospital and we wondered whether we should have a word with the soldier on duty at the time. Jim decided to stroll over and have a quiet word to put him wise. "You might want to know that two of those girls were Jerrybags and are just out of the V.D. clinic at our hospital." was Jim's quiet comment. "****off", was the reply, "They may have been *******Jerrybags before but they are now ******* Tommybags." Jim and I became a little older and wiser on that day and realised that soldiers are soldiers the world over regardless of their nationality!

Bernard had also to attend to the victualling of German naval ships, the two minesweepers and other ships in the harbour and this went on for some time. I remember, on one occasion, he sent one German naval officer packing with a flea in his ear for complaining that his men weren't getting enough fresh vegetables. A few weeks later the minesweepers were handed over to the French Navy and were sailed by their crews to Brest, St Nazaire or Lorient on minesweeping duties.

On the day that the two minesweepers left for Lorient in Brittany, the German Captains had to come to the office for their orders and charts for the voyage. One forgot to take his seven by fifty Zeiss Dienstglas service binoculars which Bern was holding for him and, as they were going spare, I had to look after them for the time being and they have made good bird watching binoculars ever since.

The naval contingent stayed on until the end of July. There were many service parties during this time and the whole Island had quite a holiday atmosphere. One of my first tasks was to go with a Scots Royal Marine driver by the name of Pollack to Springfield sports ground where many of the German Army vehicles had been accumulated. On arrival I particularly admired a small German Army D.K.W. two stroke motor cycle amongst a pile of discarded German Army vehicles. In a flash, Pollack wanted to grab it for me and put it in the back of the Humber brake in which we were travelling! I had to restrain him from doing so as I was afraid that it might cause trouble in the future, but it was tempting!

My next task turned up a day later. Bern sent for a requisitioned car with a German Army driver. The Beachmaster, one Lieutenant Commander Clarke, had arrived ashore and wished to be shown around parts of the Island to examine the sort of fortifications he would have had to cope with if the Germans hadn't surrendered. We drove to Gorey Harbour to commence with, then to Bouley Bay and then to Rozel. I was particularly gratified on arrival at Rozel Harbour as the German officer lined up his troops on our arrival and saluted

Lieut. Commander Clarke as we alighted from the car. The young officer gave me a strange look, seemed to recognise me and with a grin said "Sind sie ein padfinder?" (Are you a pathfinder?) I was quite amused, rather pleased and nodded. He had obviously recognised me from before the arrival of the liberating forces.

Lieutenant Commander Clark, the naval officer, then told me to direct the driver to go to the Underground Hospital (Now 'Jersey War Tunnels') and the centre of operations at the Battle Headquarters at St Peter's. Rather ashamedly, I hadn't a clue what he was talking about and we had to return to the Royal Yacht for further instructions to find out where these places were, before continuing with our search.

My next task was also as a guide for another German driver and a large requisitioned vehicle when it arrived outside the Royal Yacht Hotel. A senior Royal Naval officer had just arrived and wished to visit friends living in the Island. Giving instructions to the driver we first drove to Rozel Manor where we collected the lady of the manor, Madame Yvonne Riley. She then instructed me to drive to Trinity Church where we called on the Rector. I was sitting in the front with the driver but whilst waiting for the latest passenger to arrive I noticed Madame Riley surreptiously pass a large German automatic pistol to the naval officer for a souvenir. I kept my eyes ahead and pretended not to notice. We continued on a scenic drive until late afternoon when I returned all my passengers to the Manor and the Rectory and returned the vehicle to the Royal Yacht Hotel, not a little awed with the importance of my afternoon task.

A few weeks after Liberation Day we had a knock on the Exeter door and I went down to find Mrs Titcombe and son Peter, my old friends, on the doorstep and looking rather harassed. I hadn't seen them since June 1940, as they affected their hurried departure before the arrival of the Germans. Naturally we invited them in for afternoon tea and listened to a very distressing story. Mr Titcombe had died during the war and Peter and his mother had just returned to the Island to retrieve their possessions. On arrival in the Island they had been told to visit one of the administrators appointed by the States to attend to those people who, for one reason or another, had left the Island hurriedly in 1940. It appears that on requesting the return of their furnishings, silver and antiques all they were given was a bill for storage and told that their possessions had been sold off after a certain time but that the money received did not cover the storage costs and that there was nothing to come. They were naturally upset; we could do nothing to help and they left the Island a short time later in disgust and I don't know if they ever returned.

The tenants of the Stag's Head Hotel, our neighbours, had also left the Island on the last plane out in June 1940 as the landlord, a retired Army Captain from the First World War, and also on the reserve, had thought it his duty to return to England as the German Occupation of the Island was imminent. He was placed in a holding area, obtained seats on one of the last planes to leave the Airport and phoned for his wife and adopted daughter to take a taxi immediately to the Airport. They rushed quickly to the Airport with a small suitcase as instructed, the daughter with an attaché case holding a pound of Jersey butter. They then left the Island just escaping before the arrival of the Germans. At their sudden departure the brewery had given the tenancy to the barman and his wife for the time being and they were still in the hotel when the original tenants returned on the first mail boat to the Island after the Liberation. On inquiring for their business to be returned, they were told that they had forfeited their tenancy and possessions which were not returned to them when requested.

They were devastated. Their livelihood, family possessions, all disposed of for carrying out what they thought was a duty for their country. Fortunately another firm offered them licensed premises to manage, but not in the same class or position as the original. It obviously hadn't payed to return to Britain to serve their country!

In August the so called friends from the Church offered to sell their hotel to my father as they were possibly returning to the mainland. My father wasn't interested as he no longer trusted them and politely declined the offer, hoping at least that these people would offer to reimburse him for the school fees paid by our family at the beginning of the Occupation. There was no offer made, nothing of the loan on paper and Dad was too proud to ask and, I suppose, just learned a lesson.

One day in August my mother and I were just leaving the Exeter when we saw Brother Edward and his deputy, Brother Marcel, my employers from De La Salle College, The Beeches, walking down Queen Street and approaching us. When they spotted my mother and me they immediately crossed the road to chat and pass the time of day. Brother Edward asked me if I would return to teach when the school opened again in September as they were still very short of qualified teachers. I said that I would be only too pleased to do so and then he turned to my mother and told her how proud he was that so many of his old boys had joined the Forces to fight for their country and had acquitted themselves during the previous five years. My mother was naturally proud and pleased at his comments.

In the July, Roderick Dobson approached me inquiring if I would like a trip to the Ecrehous reefs which are situated roughly half way between Jersey's east coast and the coast of Normandy. He wished to check if the war had had any effect on the bird population since his last visit in 1937. As I had never been to any of the outlying islets before I jumped at the offer and arrived by bike, a German requisitioned one, at Gorey Harbour at the given time on that sunny morning in July. There were four of us to make the trip, Rods, Eric Oldham, Paddy Bertram and myself. They had borrowed a sixteen foot clinker built boat with a ten horse power Stuart Turner motor. It was a sunny day, but with a keen north-easterly breeze. We soon left the shelter of the harbour and in no time I was over the side feeding the fish. It was definitely a choppy trip and I was a rotten sailor and soon regretted my enthusiasm to make the voyage. To complete my discomfort the motor stopped running half a dozen times and we wallowed in the choppy seas while Paddy tinkered with the motor, finally getting it running again. By the time that we had arrived I was wet and miserable and had to be helped on to the shingle to recover. However, the reefs were magic, the Maitresse Ile, with its single wooden and corrugated iron hut still in reasonable condition and the Island covered with screaming nesting gulls, the numbers of which had quadrupled since before the war. The adjacent Marmotier Reef, a large single rock, covered with small stone-built fishermen's huts was relatively undamaged and very picturesque. After sandwiches and coffee I soon recovered and enjoyed every moment of the short stay on the Islands. The return trip was not as harrowing as we had a following wind and sea and the engine only packed up twice.

Our neighbours in Queen Street were a family who owned the millinery shop across the road from the pub. It was called Le Petit Louvre and as well as owning the business, they lived in a detached house on the Route du Fort (then Peel Road) which was nearly struck by one of the sticks of bombs that had straddled Fort Regent area on the evening of June 28th 1940. The owners were a Captain and Mrs

Poole and Mrs Poole's sister, Mrs Renouf. They were very patriotic people; spread the English news around from their illicit radio, an activity fraught with danger. They also had a Siamese cat by the name of Quiko who they carefully kept in, being afraid that hungry soldiers would catnap him for food! What we didn't know about them was that Captain Poole was a member of a self-formed group of ex British Army officers of the First World War who mustered together just after the arrival of the Germans and named themselves the Jersey Loyalists. He told my father that one of their objectives was to monitor the suspect behaviour of certain Islanders. Some of them were business people, some country farmers, and even certain members of the States of Jersey, people whose dealings with the German occupiers amounted to collaboration with the enemy to the extent that some of their activities were possibly treasonable.

We knew little about the activities of this little group until Captain Poole approached my father later in the year in disgust. According to him, the Home Secretary, Mr Chuter Ede, had visited the Island and had been given the dossier detailing the activities of these collaborators, expecting that these people would be brought to justice for their unpatriotic activities throughout the Occupation. These ex-Army loyalists had just been informed that, as some of the accusations were unsubstantiated and just hearsay, the whole dossier, accurate that it might have been, would only open a can of worms in the Island, that people wanted to forget the war and that further proceedings would not be carried out. Captain Poole and his group were particularly disgusted as collaborators and quislings on the Continent were being brought to justice for their wartime activities. I believe that most of the findings of this group have been kept under wraps ever since although there was a feeling in the Island of whitewash which was accentuated even more when many of the population wondered why Winston

Churchill never visited his "Dear Channel Islands". All the same, we had visits from the King and Queen, Herbert Morrison, Home Secretary, and members of the Privy Council and to cap it all, Field Marshal Montgomery. However, regardless of the rumours, nothing was done and so we will never know the truth of these allegations.

I was soon back at school and helping in the pub for the first autumn term. In early October Roderick tackled me once again. "Can you get next weekend off? On Saturday we are going to Icho Tower". This was an old fortification, originally built against the French, on a large rock and situated about two miles south of the Island. It was accessible only at low water and on the spring tides. "We are going there to fish, check out the bird population and repair any damage to the interior of the Tower caused possibly by the Germans having used the Tower for target practice during the previous five years".

I jumped at the opportunity and cycled to Le Hocq Inn as instructed at the required time. Waiting there was a lorry belonging to a farmer friend, a Mr Blandin, loaded with timber from a dismantled German hut, sheets of glass for repairing the windows, fishing nets, supplies and sleeping bags etc. We were soon on our way as the tide was low but would soon be rising. Mr Blandin drove down the Fondrion gutter through pools of sea water, gravel and seaweed. When east of Icho we turned right and were able to drive to the shingle close to the Tower. Roderick opened the iron-studded door with a massive key and we started unloading the truck quickly to let Mr Blandin return before the rapidly rising tide engulfed him and his lorry.

Our first task was to set the net across a gutter known as the Rippee. By the time that we had set the net with small boulders along the bottom, and corks across the top, the tide was around our feet and we quickly moved back to the Tower and carted the remainder of the gear inside. In the Tower there was an old four poster bed and three camp beds and the damp granite ceiling hung with small stalactites. To get on to the roof one had to climb a set of granite steps built into the interior of the massive wall.

There was an old water tank on the roof but the contents were polluted by the many gulls that rested there. Roderick and Paddy set about repairing the window frames destroyed by the German artillery with the timber we had carted out, whilst Eric Oldham created an oven with a large Smiths biscuit tin and a primus stove. He then cooked a splendid meal with a large piece of beef and vegetables but it was dark outside before we sat down to an excellent supper. By the time we had finished our meal we had to attend to the net. It was a moonlight night and as we descended the iron ladder we could see the net glistening in the shallowing water with the trapped fish.

Having emptied the substantial catch of mullet and a few other varieties of fish into boxes, we set the net again and returned to the Tower. By now I was very tired and decided to turn in. Not Roderick. At midnight he went low-water fishing in the moonlight with his hook and spike and returned a couple of hours later with three large and one medium sized lobster. I have never known a more avid low-water fisherman, a great Jersey pastime, but he wasn't even a local!

The next day was spent with the repairs to the Tower and bird watching, and I acted as a labourer to all three. Mr Blandin arrived at low tide to collect the catch and arranged to collect the other three on the next day as I had to leave at midnight to attend school on the Monday morning. That night, as soon as the tide had receded enough I set off in the moonlit shallowing sea, along the two miles of sand and shingle to Le Hocq where I had left my bike. The walk back in the moonlight was quite eerie, splashing through the salt water gutters of the Fondrion and putting up feeding waders as they would suddenly fly up with startled piping alarm calls, and I was quite relieved when I finally reached Le Hocq slipway. Quickly retrieving my bike from the backyard of the pub I was soon home, a few hours sleep and back to school, teaching on the Monday morning.

The liberating force gradually left the Island from the end of July and throughout August when their respective tasks were completed. At one time I felt a depressive feeling of anti-climax, as, after the dreadful five years of Occupation, peace had arrived and we had nothing more to look forward to.

As the war against Japan was still continuing, Bern returned to England at the end of July and was posted to Trincomalee in Ceylon. The Japanese war came to an end in August and after a short while he returned home to Britain to be demobbed and to return to his job at Barclays Bank.

Business at the Exeter was now good as many servicemen were returning to the Island with their gratuities after demobilization. My time was full with teaching at the school and helping at the pub in any spare time. I managed to enter St Luke's Teachers' Training College in Exeter in September 1946 but cut short my studies to return home early to help my father in the pub as my parents had taken on my sister's four children to rear after her sudden death at the age of twenty-seven in January 1946.

The sequel to my Occupation adventures occurred the following year in April 1946. One evening I had a phone call, once again from

Roderick. "Kevin, can you get a fortnight off sometime in mid May? I have just about completed the work on my Magnum Opus, the book on the birds of the Channel Isles. I must visit the other islands to find out if the five years of German occupation has made any difference to the bird life in these islands." "What's a Magnum Opus?" was my ignorant reply and when Rods had explained that he had been writing a book on the birds of the Channel Isles since coming to the Island in 1934 and that Magnum Opus (Major Work) was a cheeky way of referring to his work. Regardless of the consequences, I decided that I couldn't possibly miss out on this chance of a lifetime and said that I could.

For several years, Alderney, just forty miles to the north and only visible from Jersey on a clear day, had been to me just a smudge on the horizon. Today, May 21st 1946 we were to visit this island, the last in our Channel Isle bird survey. I was accompanying Roderick Dobson, friend and mentor, who was completing his book carried out during the past twelve years on the birds of the Channel Islands.

The first island we had visited was Guernsey and camping in a friend's packing shed in the Vale we were continuously serenaded by a first ever for me, the monotonous song from the now rare corncrake or landrail. Sark had taken us three days, one in teeming rain, trudging many lanes and pathways and enjoying the tranquillity of this still unspoilt island. We had also explored Herm and encircled the Island by fishing boat and landing on the many humps, some with exotic names like the Longue Pierre and Grand Amfroque that stretch to the north of that beautiful island. Now, having completed several days in Guernsey, checking every possible bay on the north-west coast, hunting for the elusive kentish plover, and hiking the wooded valleys, water lanes and south coast cliffs, we were about to visit the most northerly of the Islands.

At Guernsey airport we boarded the little seven seater, De Havilland Rapide at nine o'clock for the twenty minute flight to Alderney. It was rather cold and unpleasant to begin with, low cloud and drizzle accompanying the north-easterly breeze. This was my first flight and I was a bit apprehensive as our plane trundled across the grass runway with increasing speed and was soon into low cloud. A brief kaleidoscope of glasshouses, windmills, packing sheds and tiny fields sped past as we emerged into brilliant sunshine. Before leaving Guernsey, Roderick had quietly asked the pilot to circle Ortac, an isolated rock situated between the Casquet lighthouse and the Island, before heading for Alderney. In a few minutes we arrived over a large white-capped rock with hundreds of sea birds milling around, disturbed by the noise of our engines or afraid of this giant bird from above. I wondered if the other five passengers thought that this might be the new "scenic route" from Guernsey to Alderney but nothing was said. We took as many photographs as possible in the available time whilst circling the rock, then continued to Alderney, landing over the other gannet colony of Les Etacs, the Garden Rocks, as we touched down on the rather bumpy airstrip on the Island.

I thought that I had seen the last of the German Army a few weeks after the Liberation but when we arrived at our little guest house in the main street of St Anne we were surprised to find, a year later, German soldiers in motley uniforms working hard, repairing and rebuilding many of the houses that had been damaged and vandalised during the war. It was a strange experience, German soldiers once again. Having settled in at Mrs Rioux' Guest House and enjoying a quick coffee, we set out to explore the Island. Walking down Crabby Lane to commence with, we passed a new German bakery which was still in use. Even though the Islands were liberated at the end of the European war the Alderney people were unable to return to their island home until December 1945.

From Crabby Lane we moved down to Platte Saline Beach in our search for the rare kentish plover that had bred there in pre-war days. It was there that we were in for another shock because, in a paddock above the beach ,we came upon a large flock of sheep with three sheep dogs, a German Army shepherd, also in part uniform, an idyllic scene, but enough to send his original Sergeant-Major into a fit of apoplectic rage! A quick photo and then on to the beach itself to find at least five pairs of the rare kentish plover with eggs in their scrape of a nest. This was good news as it was obvious that the activities of the German forces had no effect on the breeding pairs. I was quite exhausted by the end of the day but there was to be no rest.

Early the next morning Roderick had organised with the local Trinity House pilot, Nick Allen to take us to the gannet colonies in the motor fishing vessel Burhou, firstly to the Garden Rocks and then to Ortac before landing us on the low-lying island called Burhou to the north west of Alderney. The sea was calm, the day sunny and warm and we were able to land on the Garden Rocks, the first people to do so since the war and arrival of the gannets. Roderick insisted that I be the first to land and we climbed to the top taking many photographs of the nesting kittewakes, razorbills, guillemots and gannets. We then sailed on to Ortac and Nick Allen was amazed that anyone could have been seasick with the sea like a millpond, but I soon changed his opinion, as, in the heat of the May sun and the smell of the diesel engine, the gentle rolling of the boat was just too much for my stomach and I succumbed. After the Gannet Rocks of Les Etacs we circled Ortac taking many photographs, the swell being too great for us to land. The last stop was the Island of Burhou with the sea around an amazing sight with thousands of those wonderful clowns of the sea, puffins, flying around and making a huge raft of them in the calm water. There were also razorbills, guillemots and cormorants, all three species of gull and all of great interest and noted in detail. Although the Island had been shelled during the war and the little stone hut destroyed, it having been used for target practice, the wartime activities had had no ill effects on the breeding colonies and even the little storm petrels were still nesting in the ruins of the damaged hut. Our friend and expert on world sea birds, R M Lockley visited the Island with Roderick in June and estimated that fifty thousand pairs of puffins were nesting in the burrows in 1946.

As for the gannet colonies on the Garden Rocks and Ortac, it seems that the first breeding gannet was discovered in June 1940 by a Major J A Wallace, keen ornithologist who had landed on Ortac just prior to the Army evacuation of Alderney. He landed to study the kittiwakes that occasionally bred on the west face. One of his men found a gannet sitting on a nest with an egg and this was the first report of a gannet nesting in the Channel Isles. They had arrived with the Germans!

There are now less than a couple of hundred puffins to be seen on Burhou during the breeding season. My own personal opinion as to why the puffins were so successful during the five years was because the Germans collected all of the gulls' eggs for food, and even after the war, to commence with, the local fishermen would land on the Island in May and June to collect buckets of gulls' eggs for their own consumption. Now, all birds on the Island are protected, the gulls have proliferated with much available food and the puffins have great difficulty in surviving. So much for thoughtless conservation. After four days on the Island we flew back to Guernsey and then by mail boat on to Jersey.

Compared with all of the other Channel Islands, Alderney had suffered from the war far more than the other islands. Apart from about half a dozen civilians the whole population had been evacuated to England on June 23rd 1940. For the war years the Island had been populated by German troops and Organization Todt engineers with the slave workers incarcerated in camps. At the end of the war it was the heaviest fortified area between the North Cape of Russia and the Spanish border!

Thus my Occupation adventures came to an end. They commenced when I was barely thirteen and ended in my nineteenth year. It had its good and bad times, the latter, mostly self inflicted. Although occupied by over thirty-six thousand troops for most of the war, the Islands must have been one of the most peaceful places in the whole of Europe and the soldiers and sailors were for the most part, disciplined and well behaved. Throughout those five years, most Islanders kept their distance from the occupying forces, avoiding fraternising with the enemy and keeping to a policy of passive resistance. Because of our unique situation there was little more that we could do.

As for our occupiers, their behaviour was far better than we could have expected. Whether the threat of being transferred to the Russian Front helped in their good behaviour was a possibility. After a few months of Occupation one might say that they had become part of the local scenery. For five long years these soldiers in field grey uniforms were constantly in evidence in town and country, quietly occupying' themselves with tasks or pleasures in hand. One other bonus was that we rarely saw any of their Forces under the influence of drink. Not that they didn't drink but their discipline was strict and leisure time spent in their own clubs and not mixing with the civilian population.

Where we were indeed fortunate was in the quiet strength of our Bailiff, Sir Alexander Coutanche and other Crown Officers, and the policy of the Island's German Commandant, General Graf Rudolf Von Schmettow, a member of the Silesian aristocracy, who, we were told, was instrumental in keeping the Gestapo from policing the Islands, and thus preventing possible atrocities during those five years, as did occur in other occupied countries.

A few months after the Liberation my mother came out with a strange comment which amused many people at the time. Her joke, "It is no good, it is so depressing, I am just putting on more weight and just can't seem lose it. We will just have to have another Occupation!" She never did lose weight and fortunately we never had another wartime Occupation.

May 1945 at St Helier Docks. Lieutenant B R Le Cocq, Captain Fremantle and Commander T Le Pirouet.

Above: Kevin and Bernard outside the Pomme D'or Hotel.

Right: Kevin and Bernard "Taking over the Royal Yacht Hotel as a billet", May 12th 1945.

Above: The Royal Marine contingent, Force 135, outside the Southampton Hotel, St Helier.
Below: One for the album. The Le Cocq Family, May 12th 1945 at the Exeter Inn, Queen Street.

Top: Troop ship Royal Ulsterman in St Aubin's Bay, May 12th 1945.
Middle and Bottom: The Royal Navy contingent Force135 leaving Jersey in July 1945. Task completed!

May 21st 1946 during Kevin's trip to Alderney.
Above: A German POW shephard.
Below: Kevin "liberates" a large German gun emplacement at Giffoine.

Back To The Tranquil Isle

S ixty-five years have flown by since the euphoric few weeks following the Liberation of the Islands in the May and June of 1945.

During the five years of German occupation the Islands had been transformed from a peaceful tourist haven with agriculture as its primary industry to become one of the strongest fortified areas in the whole of Europe. This little group of islands was the only part of Great Britain to be occupied by the Germans and Hitler was determined never to relinquish them. In consequence they were not liberated until after his death on the 30th April 1945.

Evidence of this five year military occupation are still to be observed throughout the Islands, the massive bunkers and fortifications of steel and re-enforced concrete still evident, both on the coast and inland and impossible to eradicate. Where they stand they are as important to our history as our more ancient and beautiful castles like Mont Orgueil and Elizabeth Castle and the many other forts built in the past for the defence of the Island. Some, like the famous underground hospital are now tourist attractions and visited annually by scores of people from all over Europe.

Many German soldiers have, in the meantime brought their families to holiday in the Islands and to show them where they were stationed during the war. The Island commandant, General Graf Rudolf von Schmettow was treated as an honoured guest when he returned to Jersey after the war, the Islanders showing their appreciation of his governing leniency during his time as Island commandant.

I had an amusing experience while working at the St Helier Yacht Marina on one occasion in the late nineteen eighties. I had arrived on duty for the night shift at ten o'clock one evening. A little later a large German sailing yacht arrived, crewed by four rather elderly German yachtsmen. Having moored up they came to the office to pay their dues. While in the office one asked me if there was anywhere to enjoy a drink at that late hour. I told them, that, as yachtsmen they would be welcome at St Helier Yacht Club and proceeded to instruct them how to get there, and off they went. Just after twelve, the four returned in a rather jolly mood and came into the office to thank me for giving them the instructions as to how to get to the club. As they were about to return to their boat for the night, one passed the comment, "I think that your Mrs Thatcher is correct in defending your possessions in the Falkland Islands, if you don't mind my saying so" and then, as an afterthought said, with a smile, "You had better be careful in case the French don't attempt the same". I just couldn't resist a grin and comment in reply "No, I don't really think so, that was tried in 1940 and you know what happened then!" The four returned to their yacht, chortling away, highly amused having quickly seen the point! It is a remote possibility that they were part of the occupying force of Kriegesmarine (Navy) in the early forties! They were the right age.

I gave up the tenancy of the Exeter at Christmas 1968, our family having tenanted these licensed premises since 1980 or thereabouts, a total in excess of eighty years. We had been proud of this fact but family illness and because the pub, the only one in the main street of St Helier, was becoming extremely difficult to manage in its present form and with the conditions imposed by the brewery, it was no longer for us a viable business. My father and I no longer considered it worth the worry, effort and commitment necessary to manage these licensed premises. By this time it was necessary to give in my notice and change to more congenial and satisfying occupations.

My father died in the spring of 1975, having been a highly popular landlord at the Exeter where he had spent a great deal of his life, that is, from 1925 until Christmas 1968. Faith and I continued to live in the Island until 1992, including the management for five years at the old family home of Old Bank Guest House in Gorey Village. After Gorey I tried many occupations including fishing with my own boat for five years at La Rocque and then, in 1982, I was offered my all time favourite job at the new Saint Helier Harbour yacht marina which was opened that year. I enjoyed this position until my retirement age in 1991. We then decided to join our two daughters in Western Australia in the autumn of that year. We have been in Albany, South West Australia, in the same house since that time.

Roderick Dobson, my mentor and close friend, returned to his wife's country of Australia with their family within a year or so of the Liberation and as soon as there were available travel places on the liners at that time. He completed his book, "Birds of the Channel Isles," from that country and proceeded to study the dragonflies of Eastern Australia. He was an avid and meticulous collector, discovering many new species and finally donated his collection to the Canberra Natural History Museum. They showed their gratitude by financing another expedition to study the insects and bird life of Eastern Australia for their natural history department. He tried many times to persuade me to join him in that country and offered to sponsor me for that purpose, but I was tied to the family and the pub and was unable to go. He died in Jersey well before our decision to emigrate and he never knew that soon I would be watching species different to those he had taught me to recognise during those wartime days in Jersey.

My brother Bernard who continued with his profession at Barclays Bank until his retirement, is still going strong and we hope to visit the Island once again this summer to celebrate his ninetieth birthday. Needless to say, our conversation will turn to those wonderful few weeks when Captain Fremantle, Commander T Le B Pirouet, their secretary, Lieutenant(S) Bernard Le Cocq, and their officers and men of the Royal Navy and marines of Force 135 returned to the Island on May 12th 1945 for the Liberation and to celebrate the end of "My Favourite Occupation". It was so because I was young, life was exciting and I had everything to look forward to. What more could one desire?

There were many smaller invasions of the Islands subsequent to the Occupation, but mainly by invitation. Firstly there were the Welsh girls to work in the potato stores. Then, during the late 1940s and early 1950s, Breton workers came to do vital work on the farms. About the same time a trickle of Italian and German hotel workers were arriving before larger numbers of very welcome Portuguese and Madeirans who came to work in the burgeoning tourism industry.

In the 1960s the world banking fraternity invaded the Islands to avail themselves of the monetary advantages which had been bestowed on the Islands in the past by two rather dissolute British monarchs. The first was King John of Magna Carta fame. The Channel Isles stayed loyal to the English crown when John lost his French possessions to the French king, and this included the neighbouring region of Normandy. Later, during the Civil War, young Charles Stuart, heir to the English throne, escaped from Southern England to Jersey to be made welcome and safe from Oliver Cromwell's Roundheads. He later rewarded the Islanders with certain privileges for their loyalty to the Royalist cause during the civil war.

With the great increase in the finance industry came prosperity but also inflation and a large increase in population, the Island's numbers expanding to nearly double of what they had been during the Occupation by the German forces.

It was My Favourite Occupation because I, a rather grumpy old ex-pat Crapaud, liked it that way and prefer to remember our beautiful Islands before the inevitable march of progress, necessary though it had to be. I enjoyed the wartime pace of life and the peace and slow progress that was the norm at that time. We finally found it in the little port city of Albany on the beautiful south coast of Western Australia.

Then and now. Kevin and Bernard stand in exactly the same spot 60 years later. Kevin with the Fire Engine that put out the fire at Norman's after the air raid on 28th June 1940.